ROOTED

RootEd

How Trauma Impacts Learning and Society

S.R. ZELENZ

Z.C.G.

CONTENTS

~ 1 ~

PREFACE

"We need this insight."
Mike Kernell, Board Member,
Shelby County Schools, Tennessee (Memphis)

This work came to fruition during my doctoral dissertation process. My initial inquiry when beginning my doctoral journey was to find out why the child was removed from education. Why do they not see the child? The reason this was important to me is personal. I began having challenges with the school system as a parent. This actually began even earlier than the school system, with the daycares my oldest child was enrolled in during the 1990's. Much of the tactics used by said daycares were what I considered abuse. However, as the parent, they spoke down to me as if the reason they had to treat my child in such a manner was my fault. They would then point out that they had my child more than I did, so they knew my child better than I did. All this told me was that the behavior issues they were having had to be a direct result of their interactions with my child if they had my child more than I did. The constant attacks received as a parent did not stop when my child entered the public school system.

1

As early as kindergarten, my child was being removed from the classroom and ostracized from the learning environment. Teachers were telling me to utilize punishment and reward systems. They were encouraging me to drug my child so he could comply with their limited restrictions. I had resisted the drugging aspect until he was in 3rd grade. The attacks on my child only continued to grow as he aged, even after he was drugged for the school system's needs. So, I became a teacher to find out why. I have since completed a master's in education and doctorate in educational leadership and change (short of full completion of the dissertation. I ran out of funding). This work was a personal determination to finish my doctoral research and find the solutions I was desperately seeking for my son, who is now a young adult.

It may be too late for my first-born child, but my second and third children were raised differently based upon the research I have done for this book. I can personally attest that absolutely none of the issues faced with my first child are present in my other two children and I firmly believe it has everything to do with what I have done in my research. I did expose these other two children to the public school system in short spurts and it did not take long before the attacks on my children began. My youngest was attacked within the first 2 weeks of kindergarten by the teacher. He has not been in a public school since.

My children do not demonstrate any of the behavioral issues that are so common in public schooled children. They are incredibly respectful, kind, considerate, responsible, eager to accomplish their goals, serious researchers, and what most people consider normal childhood behavior issues (or teen behavior issues) are non-existent with them. Having raised a child the traditional way and then having a second chance with children born 12-13 years after my first born and doing it very differently and carefully researched, I can say that it definitely is the belief system in the current educational system that is ruining our children. This includes parenting that is reinforced by schools and "parent" experts who support authoritarian derived parent-child domination.

I did teach in the public school system for two decades, and I worked with thousands of children. That journey into teaching also showed me the way in which teachers spoke to children on a regular basis. I was also exposed to their negative and derogatory banter about children in their classrooms and in the teacher's lounge. I am not saying there weren't good teachers or good administrators, but the good ones were frequently attacked by other teachers and the administration as a whole. It is difficult to be a teacher who cares for the emotional development of children in a public school system. I can't speak for private schools, but I would assume it is quite similar since they all derive from the same educational belief system that began in the 1850's.

This research was derived from personal experience as a parent and as a teacher. My interest in brain development and psychology became paramount as it is very clear that our school systems do not take these aspects into consideration. They have been using the same behavioral conditioning models that were created at the turn of the 20th century. The only change that has occurred since that time is the increase of propaganda material to direct minds to focus on what those in power determined was important. Those who make these decisions were very frequently not experts in the field. They were those in a position of influence in their communities and had their own goals for schooled outcomes.

Many could easily attest that the focus of the curriculum has left out many voices and it is frequently labeled as racist. I personally feel that all ethnicities were abolished in our curriculum and that the goal was to create a unified nation that would have the same beliefs.

I can see how they thought this would be beneficial to prevent individual cultural groups from fighting one another.

Working in a melting pot country like this creates challenges not present in one culture societies. Comparing the educational outcomes of a melting pot country with one that has an individual culture is highly unfair to the students. Erasing their identity is epigenetically traumatic and has clearly been unsuccessful. We only need to look around us to see the fallout from this decision. European Americans have little to no awareness of their own individual ancestral heritages and they treat European cultures as fantasy or something to mock. Many are attacked for attempting to maintain their cultural identities or their ancestry as it goes against the manufactured curriculum designed to align with a generic western European high ideal. Even within western Europe, this is not in alignment with who they are. It's a manufactured identity with carefully sculpted stories that were designed to make the students believe certain things about "others" and to keep their eyes focused on how "others" are the enemy.

Later education attempted more cultural inclusion, but really only treated it as some kind of fantasy observation. The mere treatment of ancestral cultural traditions as things of the past is quite peculiar since these very traditions are practiced in their native countries to this day. They were only erased in melting pot countries with the intention of moving society away from their identities and toward the direction of the purveyors of the education system's goals.

I am not saying the issues with my children were in direct correlation with this aspect, but it is a huge aspect worthy of consideration. I know for myself; I know little about my ancestral heritage. Same with my children. We are a mix of various European cultures, but we have no identity. We are a generic "White" group now. That feels entirely soulless to me, and it has spurned me to take my younger children around the world to be exposed to cultures in their native lands in order to see what normal cultural behavior looks like. I do believe this has had a significant impact on the way that my own children perceive others and themselves. They do not feel threatened by any other culture, and they try hard to be respectful and considerate of their traditions, customs, and beliefs. We can discuss what we see and how the behaviors of those we come into contact with align with their beliefs, their cultural identity, and their current environment. This has also allowed us to review the behaviors witnessed in our own country of birth, the United States of America. After several years of traveling globally, we can honestly say that it is incredibly obvious to us the grand degree to which Americans are in pain due to the treatment of their individual cultural identities and the way in which they have been programmed by the education system. It has created a society that is eager to abuse and is incredibly selfish. To behave in a manner that honors others is to also find oneself attacked. This should be alarming to citizens. A unified nation should not abuse one another to create a manufactured identity.

I think what should be more pressing at this juncture is the impact of that constant abuse on the psychological development of our youth and how that manifests in each generation. What kind of society are we creating with these efforts? It is far more than cultural identity lost. It is loss of personal healthy boundaries, respect of self and others, and the courage to take on great challenges without fear. We have crippled our society. The amount of money spent on our current education system has not produced a higher educated society either. Only those who had a vested interest in learning the material truly do learn. The rest learn how to manipulate the system and others in order to achieve undeserved gains. This has created a society of abusers and systems that ensure that the abuse cycle continues. Those who have grown up in it do not even realize they are in it. That is how abuse works. It becomes normalized.

~ 2 ~

INTRODUCTION

IT IS SAID THAT THE ONLY WAY TO HEAL IS THROUGH CONFRONTING YOUR PREDATOR. THE PURPOSE OF THIS BOOK IS TO CONFRONT THE PREDATOR. ONLY THEN CAN OUR SOCIETY BEGIN TO HEAL.

Dangerous Society

IT ISN'T THE RAPING ITSELF THAT CAUSED THE DEEPEST TRAUMA. IT WAS THE TREATMENT BY SOCIETY AFTER THE RAPE THAT TRAUMATIZED THE MOST. IT WAS AS IF THE PREDATOR MARKED THE VICTIM FOR THE "TRIBE" TO KNOW WHO TO ATTACK.

One does not need to look very far to find evidence of how dangerous society has become. The rise in predatory behavior is unprecedented and the parallel rise in people standing up against their oppressors and predators is astounding. There is hope, yet there is still much to be understood if we are to ever see a healthy transition for our future society.

That is what this book is about. The "predator" wasn't so much the people who did the initial violation. The real predator was the

7

society and how they reacted and responded to the victim after the trauma. That is far more traumatizing.

Many prefer judgment, ostracizing, and financial, physical, or verbal attack on the victim for having been victimized. Healing from trauma requires a deep understanding of it. Victims are then placed in responsibility for understanding their trauma as well as understanding the predatory behavior done to them. Only then can they move forward in a healthy manner that prevents further trauma. This is difficult for many to obtain.

This book is also to help those involved in raising future generations to realize their complicity in perpetuating predatory behavior and further victimization. It is widely known that abuse happens in a cycle. Abusers create more abusers. Abusers also create victims. Some victims become abusers. Some victims remain victims because they had no outside support to help them navigate the trauma that was inflicted upon them. How many of those victims become future abusers is also in the hands of those in position to change the trajectory for them, and ultimately everyone that person has contact with for the rest of their lives.

> *The tribe learned to control their violence by finding a common scape-goat to take their violence out on.*
>
> *~ Rene Girard*

The System

The embedded narcissism in the system is about control and control through emotions is one more arm of that. What results is a transfer of focus from one to another and neither encourages independence and stability. People will be unstable after challenging their beliefs and want to be told what to do and how. This book will offer clear examples and suggestions to help them with this process. Adaptation to new understanding destabilizes and requires serious introspection. Dismantling of one's conditioning can be psychologically challenging for many and the goal is not to create a new form of dependence for them.

This book is written using scientific terms and theories based upon actual research studies. Their use is to substantiate any points made and this book will refrain from using softer language often found in self-help guidebooks. The language choice is done so that clarity, effectiveness, and practicality can be embraced and implemented with little obstruction to comprehension. It needs to be clear. It needs to be unemotional. It needs to encourage independence. It needs to offer clear guidance that is paired with self-sufficiency reinforcement.

Codependency is trained in our schools and family structures. Codependency and narcissistic reactions are dangerous. The goal of education should liberate people. Only then can we have true democracy.

Dictatorships

In researching different countries that have experienced dictatorships, we find a commonality of corruption in their post-dictatorship governments. There is a community-wide mistrust of government. People learned to live in secret under the dictatorship, thus they learn to skirt all rules to survive. It's no different than living with an authoritarian parent. Teenagers will sneak around to do what they want despite the authority limiting them. They learn to lie to survive and learn how to be duplicitous to function under the "rule" and still "live." Absolute power really does corrupt absolutely. It seems exceedingly difficult to truly have a healthy democracy after entire generations are raised under such control. Their minds are not capable of thinking differently. They have been programmed and will continue to react accordingly.

Empowering dictators happens by fearing them. In fact, that is why dictators incite fear of them. This fear is balanced with providing soothing words or efforts to ensure the populace aligns with the dictator as their protector. This power cannot be achieved without the control of others. The same can be said about anyone in a position of power who seeks total devotion, total adherence, total obedience, and total control. These are a larger scope of behaviors identified in the American Psychological Association's DSM manual, and all of them are rooted in one common denominator - narcissism.

Tribes

Tribal people lived in a naturally developed hypervigilant state. They learned that survival depended upon continuous awareness of their surroundings. The difference between this kind of hypervigilance and trauma-induced hypervigilance is that those raised in tribes were taught to be aware and taught what to do when they encounter danger. Those who developed hypervigilance from trauma have not been given any constructive advice. They are left in a state of fear and given no guidance on how to navigate the situation outside of manipulation from the source of the fear. This is when any number of maladaptive behaviors are developed. Coping strategies such as flight, fight, fawn, or freeze manifest in this state. The challenge lies with how society has perpetuated reactive hypervigilance. Rather than teaching survival, it has become a means of abuse and control.

Education

Our education system was designed to provide factory workers for the industrial revolution. Schools were not compulsory until 1856. Those who needed factory workers met their needs by having the government enforce compliance to provide for those needs. There is much more that will be discussed on this topic in further chapters.

What is more important to note at this juncture is that the implementation of factory schooling was also the beginning of the demise of the family and their influence on their own children. Allegiance to the school and the state (mandatory attendance) took precedence over family needs and the needs of the child.

More importantly, it also changed the way that people raised their children. Parenting shifted from producing productive family members to producing productive students who learn how to take orders and operate within compliance of the school's expectations. Nowhere in this model was emotional development considered. The awareness of the trauma induced on the child in order to maintain this compliance was never questioned.

Simultaneous implementation of the Indian Boarding Schools influenced the universal stripping of culture(s). There is significant focus on how abusively the Native American peoples were treated by the American government forcing their children into boarding schools. These schools were designed to strip them of their cultural heritage, mother tongue, and cultural identity. However, a less obvious version was simultaneously happening in the White schools and boarding schools for African Americans. One can see how the overall psyche of the United States citizen is one of distrust and hatred toward anyone who shows loyalty to their cultural heritage. This failure to adhere to the "accepted" American narrative prescribed through the education system and its focus on how to celebrate American holidays is aggressively addressed to this day. Only in recent years have people begun to challenge this exclusionary focus. People today are unaware of how this was intentionally designed to create a uniform workforce and a society conformed to one predetermined identity. In essence, cultural annihilation of all peoples was the goal. Creation of a new identity that can be controlled was the purpose.

Behavior

Rude behavior is one of two things: a psychological disorder that cannot be helped or a need to be heard. Sometimes even within the psychological disorder it is still the need to be heard. If someone is shouting over them, threatening them in any way, enforcing some kind of smothering force on their being (this can include psychological smothering or manipulation) only exacerbates the issue. This frequently leads to reactionary behavior such as school shootings, rape, destruction of property, and many other antisocial behaviors. It is short-sighted to place all of these reactionary behaviors on the mentally ill. Most get to this extreme reaction after attempting to be heard by those who don't listen. Instead they are met with behaviors designed to control them and dismiss their experience. Humans are tremendously creative in finding ways to say, "You don't matter." In the end, they will be heard.

Anger is the result of feeling helpless. This is tied to having outsiders take control over another's experience. This is identical to predators dominating and threatening anyone who dares to stand up against them. The same is true when people or organizations threaten survival of those they impact if those impacted do not behave or do exactly what that person or organization demands of them and do so immediately (no room for actual reality to be considered - cold policies).

If the teacher is feeling anger, they are feeling helpless. If the natural reaction to that is to become bigger, scarier, and more dominant to "harness" control, they are using the fight response. This scares the students, makes them not trust the teacher (or authority figure), instills a fear that cannot be easily overcome by those who are already conditioned by abuse, and it makes the students dissociate.

This literally eradicates the learning platform. There may be the few who respond to this due to conditioning at home. Some of the best students are just as likely to be abused as the worst students are. Some use music and books to escape reality. They dissociate by going into other worlds that can be picked up anytime and anywhere. This is another reason why the arts matter so much.

Also, abusers use this strategy to garner control. They fear being out of control. They fear what will happen to them. So, if the person (or people) impacting them are not creating a safe space, then they will test and push to see if the person (or people) are truly trustworthy and safe. If they feel the person (or people) are unsafe, they will take that control into their own hands so they can feel safe again. How they accomplish this control is what is more worrisome without a healthy role model teaching them what healthy self-control is. They will be abusive to gain that sense of safety.

When dealing with students who behave in abusive manners, it is important to understand this core component. Behavior disorder or not, this is a critical factor and if not acknowledged, the behavior will be exacerbated by intervention "control" systems such as awards, punishments, and "discipline" models. In this book, I will address how schools are playing a role in traumatizing many students further.

We are creating ticking time bombs not only for school shootings, but also adults who cannot handle life. They may find healthier experiences after school ends or they may carry that trauma with them. This can manifest as a need to dominate, usurp, or cause harm to others who may have done nothing but resemble a previous wound. This may be a need to see punishment served in some manner. They received no justice nor acknowledgement for what happened to them. They may recreate similar situations, or they dominate to obtain the control they never had as a child. This can be found in every work environment.

Schools

Healthy boundaries are not possible in schools as they are now. Students are forced to hand their boundaries over at the door in schools. This also happens in many work environments. Schools allow children to violate one another and adults violate the students' boundaries. The students aren't allowed boundaries to protect them from adults in schools and in many "traditional" American households. When people are raised without boundaries, they violate others, or they are violated easily. They are prepared for predatory behavior.

The same is true in classrooms. Student rebellion is a predictable response to boundary violation. Many parents and teachers say "rebellion" is a normal part of development, when in fact it is a direct result of having one's boundaries disrespected and violated. Rebellion is undeveloped boundaries trying to find footing.

In Conclusion

After having taken a small stroll through the varying factors at work, we will now delve into the deeper implications suggested in this introduction. This will include more specific details relating to education, teaching, parenting, and schools. It will also include more in-depth investigation on trauma, epigenetic trauma inheritance, neuroscience relating to trauma, and psychology.

~ 3 ~

THE PROBLEM

General Problem

If the purpose of education is to help individuals and society live in healthy, balanced ways that lead to a joyful, peaceful existence, then contemporary education and most school reform efforts are failing (Jacobs, 2003). One of the reasons for this problem relates to cultural and educational hegemony and how the powers that control education seem to be aiming at conformity to a particular image of how things should be. "Educational leaders have tried to transform immigrant newcomers and other "outsiders" into individuals who matched their idealized image of what an "American" should be" (Tyack & Cuban, 1995).

I propose a radically different approach to school reform, one that recognizes the phenomenon of epigenetics and the understanding of brain development for those exposed to trauma. The latter provides a more natural model for balanced diversity and happiness (Bracho, 2006) and the former offers a scientific explanation for both why people whose DNA still reflects historical trauma are "failing" so often in modern schools and how all peoples can "redirect" DNA toward higher potentials by changing how things are done. Epigenetics, and a component of it referred to as "transgenerational epigenetic inheritance," suggests that environmental habits, from stress and diet to lifestyle choices and educational systems, can not only modify genetic expression in health and behaviors within one lifetime, but that such changes also can be passed onto offspring. My hypothesis is that modern influences on education have drastically changed or are significantly challenging more natural genetic expressions of humans in ways that contribute to the growing problems both in schools and in the world at large. I argue that recognizing this possibility and returning to what can be described as holistic ways of knowing that remain in our genes, can help reverse these problems. At the very least, it may help those whose genes themselves tend to resist most mainstream approaches to education because their epigenetic coding is closer to its original patterns.

Many classrooms disregard personal authenticity, exploration of self, and almost always employ the use of a hierarchical structure that tends to remove the opportunity for students to learn self-direction through intrinsic motivation. Learning and classroom management, the organization and maintaining of an environment conducive to learning, seldom involve self-motivated responsibility on the part of students as is commonplace in traditional Indigenous education. The following is a sample listing of issues that schools are not addressing adequately:

- Loss of interest in learning school curriculum (Kridel, 2010).
- Violence and problems of bullying (Centers for Disease Control and Prevention, 2011).

- Inadequate curricula (Rutowski, 2001) including lack of appropriate education relating to ecological issues (Slattery, 2006).
- Apathy in civic and community involvement (Marbeley & Dawson, 2009).

I offer a preliminary argument using theoretical research from a variety of fields. My hope is that this book will begin a dialogue that will move toward more experimental research. I believe the problems demand a radical rethinking of educational reform. Current educational reform, as I will show, is narrowing the focus of education and moving away from a more natural, holistic way of being in the world that was practiced by our Indigenous ancestors and continues to be practiced by many Indigenous groups, as I seek to critically examine and illustrate in this book.

By "holistic education" I refer to an approach that Ron Miller defines as a community connection that facilitates identity discovery and intrinsic respect for learning and life (Miller, 2000). The focus of this form of education is to bring about the fullest possible development of each individual in a manner that offers them the opportunity to personally experience life and their goals completely (Forbes, 2003). "Holistic education broadens and deepens the educational process. It represents a planned approach that encourages personal responsibility, promotes a positive attitude to learning and develops social skills. These are essentials in the modern world in which we live" (Hare, 2010, p. 7). As I will argue later, Indigenous ways of knowing embrace this holistic approach (or perhaps, vice-versa).

In this chapter, I will discuss the wider implications of our current reform strategies, the history of education in the United States, understanding from a systemic level, authoritarian structure and its place in the overall systems, the purpose of education and of course how this compilation of issues affect students in our public schools. These issues must be addressed to inform our current educational reform strategies.

Contemporary Education

A brief overview of how contemporary education, including reform efforts, seems to be the antithesis of holistic education will help describe the problem at a more superficial level than I will describe in later chapters. "Education as Enforcement: The Militarization and Corporatization of Schooling" offers a poignantly graphic general description of current trends. One of the contributors to this text writes:

> The school as a public good has been transformed into either a training ground for a consumer society or a pipeline for channeling disposable populations into the grim confines of the criminal justice system......Jean-Marie Durand states that "youth is no longer considered the world's future, but as a threat to its present. Vis-á-vis youth, there is no longer any political discourse except for a disciplinary one." In this discourse, both "the figure of the child and the cultural capital of youth" are being radically configured as to undermine the rights young people have as rights-bearing citizens. (Giroux, 2010, pp vii-viii)

Indeed, today's schooling does these things with consistency and schools and teachers are being held accountable for ensuring such oppressive education is successful. If the teachers cannot produce students who perform well on the standardized exams, then they are often released from their positions or the school is penalized through government take-over or funding reduction.

Loss of interest in curricula, violence, and bullying in schools are serious concerns that affect graduation rates. "Dropout rates among the population ages 16 to 24 declined between 1972 and 2008, from 15 to eight percent. However, wide disparities by race persist" (Child Trends Databank, 2010). Verification of the racial disparities' statistics can be found on the National Center for Education Statistics website. Dropout students do not have many employable skills (Child Trends Databank, 2010). Public schools focus on academic skills, without teaching these students applicable skills (Child Trends Databank, 2010). Nearly half of the dropouts are currently not in the workforce (National Center for Education Statistics, 2008). It should not be surprising that many of these dropouts live in extreme poverty and demonstrate a higher risk to be more involved in crime (Child Trends Databank, 2010).

The 2017 National Assessment of Educational Progress test results released by the United States Department of education, stated that 67% of American public school eighth graders were not proficient in math and 65% were not proficient in reading (NAEP, 2017). Urban districts bore even lower percentages. Some districts had proficiency levels ranging between 7-14%. One of the initial purposes in establishing public education in the mid-1800's was to ensure that the "three R's" were being learned: reading, writing, and arithmetic. At that point in time, eighth grade was the furthest most students ever attended school. It appears that whatever the initial goals were, 160 years later, they are not being met at the most basic level.

Race to the Top (2011) is a recent educational reform model, intended to motivate teachers, school districts, and states to raise the level of quality education, data collection and graduation results to a higher standard. No education reform strategy has researched the ability of teachers or administrators to truly empathize with their students. Teachers and administrators come from various walks of life, few of them have experienced dire poverty in their lifetimes. Higher on the pyramid we find superintendents who live completely different lives from those of the students they are responsible for. Psychology professors at University of California, Berkeley conducted a research study suggesting a person's social class dictates their ability to empathize. More specifically, this study clarified that those from upper class experience had less empathy than those who live in the lower social classes. The study stated that those in survival mode have learned how to rely on one another to survive, whereas those in the upper social classes are financially independent, and less likely to seek assistance to attend to their immediate needs. This lack of "need" for assistance is what hinders their ability to empathize with those in need (Kraus, et al., 2010). This is important to consider in our current reform strategies.

Attempts to restructure schools have aligned themselves with the hiring of extremely wealthy businessmen and women as the heads of the educational reform. Not only have they not lived the same experiences as those they oversee educating, but their ancestors most likely experienced a better life as well. The students who are not faring well in our schools are most often poor. Wealthy educators (or administrators) are most likely not prepared to relate to these students at a level which would encourage their highest learning.

School Reform: History

Our current educational system was designed to create a specific type of worker who is also a consumer to function in and drive today's capitalistic society. Public schools were originally established to assist the industrial age in its need for obedient workers who would endure long hours of repetitive, non-thinking, non-problem solving, and non-creative work. This training approach presupposed that no one in the working class was capable of individualistic, creative solutions to the problems that society faced (Gatto, 2001).

This same desire to use education to create obedient workers and compliant citizens ignored the value of diversity and tended to oppress individuals who were not white, male, and from relatively wealthy families. As John Taylor Gatto states in his book as seen edited in Ode Magazine:

> Mass schooling of a compulsory nature was conceived and advocated throughout most of the 19th century. The reason given for this enormous upheaval of family life and cultural traditions was, roughly speaking, threefold: to make good people, to make good citizens, to make each person his or her personal best. (Gatto, 2008, p. 24)

In practice, the school structure becomes more divisive and exclusive than it appears. An early forerunner of this 19th century educational purview was Dr. Alexander Inglis, Professor of Education at Harvard University, Cambridge. In his Principles of Secondary Education, he demonstrates conclusively that industrial age education was designed to segregate the under-classes (Inglis, 1918). Ranking students according to test scores, labeled children, thereby determining their future chances of success. Unfortunately, this practice continues today.

In compliance with the 2001 "No Child Left Behind" Act, students are required to test in certain mandatory subjects at predetermined grade levels. Through this form of evaluation, schools are theoretically more aware of their weaknesses, and therefore able to address areas in need of improvement. This governmental regulation ties school funding to school performance. If schools under-perform, their funding is cut. Most often, the schools that under-perform are those in lower income communities. Reduction in funding to these schools further hurts the educational prospects of students who are already at a recognized disadvantage in their living environment and socioeconomic status (Mathison & Ross, 2004).

Dr. Alexander Inglis, Assistant Professor of Education at Harvard University in 1918, wrote six basic functions of education. The perpetual continuation of Inglis' ideas merits further consideration, especially when considered as the basis for the traditional pedagogical model or system. Inglis demonstrates his idea of the six basic functions of modern schooling as the following:

1. The adjustive/adaptive function – fixed reaction to authority.
2. The integrative function – students conforming to the expectations of authority figures.
3. The diagnostic and directive function – students' records used to determine "who" the students are and what they will become.
4. The differentiating function – students are "trained" to their "diagnostic and directive function" determination and no further.

5. The selective function – utilizing Darwin's theory of evolution (1871), students with poor grades are selectively excluded from higher educational opportunities. Their peers are also very aware of these "labels" and act accordingly.

6. The propaedeutic function – the small fraction who make it through the labeling process with the highest marks are chosen to rule the most influential and controlling organizations in the country (1918).

With the concepts discussed in Inglis' writing, the goal of public school education becomes much clearer. Standardized examinations are still used to separate the abilities of the students. More importantly, these tests systematically fail to inculcate critical thinking skills and instead tend to create mass consumer mentalities, more likely to follow the trends set before them.

Although this may not have been consciously intended by those who implement these efforts, it has become the effect. To understand how we got to this place in our educational beliefs, we must understand the history behind it. Our government is an oligarchic plutocracy, this means that money decides who is in control. It is the proverbial golden rule of capitalism: whoever has the gold makes the rules. Therefore, those with money often do not attend public school. They either have private tutors or attend private schools, which teach them a different perspective of the world; their place in it and challenges them to find creative solutions to the world's problems – in effect to be our leaders. Keeping the masses in their place with a coercive education ensures that power remains with the few. These "few" have no desire to change this system for fear of losing what they have. This prevents them from doing anything to alleviate the socio-economic damages created by the inequalities in our educational system. I would now like to reiterate my point regarding current trends in administrative choices. Billionaires and company CEOs from a higher socio-economic reality are now at the helm of the educational pyramid (Fertig, 2010).

Our educational structure is a suppressive form of hierarchy. An administrator suppresses the teachers who suppress the students -- creating obedient employees. This need for control, or power, stems from the elite of our capitalistic society. This imbalance in societal structure has created strife among peoples for centuries. This is the normal structure for colonized societies. It is not the normal structure for many tribal cultures (Reagan, 2005).

School Reform: Current Reform Trends

Classes are divided up by specific subjects. Teachers are hired and expected to be experts in their "specific" area of study. The teacher's ability to cross-educate among other disciplines is not usually considered. The students' ability to see the greater picture of how the various subjects integrate into their current lives, into the history of their current world, and how everything is interconnected is rarely discussed or addressed. Everything is segregated.

It follows, then, with this kind of rigid thinking and the attendant unrealistic expectations that are the inevitable outcome of viewing children as machines, that discipline and enforced order become tantamount to success. So much so, that anything (or anyone) who questions the prevailing order or refuses to abide by its strictures is perceived as a threat to be subjected to discipline, the linchpin of coercive education. Which brings me to discuss discipline as a form of repression.

Disciplinary structures create behavior that is reminiscent of prisons. Students who do not "behave" in a certain predetermined fashion can be labeled and encouraged or compelled to seek counseling and medication. They are most often isolated to various corners of the classroom or removed entirely from the classroom. This "disciplinary" action is counterintuitive to the reform efforts guaranteeing quality education for all students in our public schools. The government requires that students attend school, but they don't guarantee that a student will actually learn anything there. Our teacher training programs continue to emphasize the same assertive discipline methodology used for decades. Teachers are not conforming to the student. If the student does not conform, he or she is excluded, leaving classroom populations that are not reflective of the diversity in the community.

Furthermore, the curriculum is written from the viewpoint of the dominant population's perspective. All other students are expected to accept this information without question. The only requirement is that they must be able to repeat this information in the manner that was given to them for the standardized test. No critical thinking is required, allowed, or even tolerated. The dominant population has also recently "edited" their history books to reflect history in a manner that they feel is important for children to believe. Texas has almost completely removed the civil rights movement from their current history textbooks (Elfman, 2010). Arizona has banned ethnic studies (James, 2010). Other states have followed similar "curriculum adjustments."

Students who come from less represented cultures are not given the opportunity to learn or share their ancestral histories and viewpoints from the same segments of history. Understandably, this creates resentment and rebellion in students, inadvertently creating the apparent need for more discipline to ensure continuing order in the classroom. This trend snowballs with the attempted imposition of ever greater discipline which is continually thwarted by behavioral challenges from kids whose educational needs are continually going unmet. A feedback loop is created that fails to realize that the very problems it was created to solve are in turn caused by the actual system itself. Suppression of inquisition and challenging of authority is not tolerated.

School Reform: Systemic Understanding

The theory behind segregation of subject matter was to isolate the core aspects that make it exist. By understanding the core aspects, the whole subject is then more completely understood. This segregation of subject matter fails to introduce the inter-relatedness each subject shares with another subject and how it applies to the world we live in. Students cannot understand the implications of these subjects in their world if the subjects are segregated from reality and the students are never taught how to look at each subject in relation to another. "Fragmentary thought has led to a widespread range of crisis, social, political, economic, ecological, psychological, etc., in the individual and in society as a whole" (Bohm, 1980, p.21). This understanding has begun to take root in the corporate world and in general management and leadership training. Corporations are paying thousands of dollars to hire specialists to assist their employees in becoming more cooperative, more constructive, and to be more efficient. A system that no longer fragments and separates is emerging. When one group does not understand what the other group does, inefficiency occurs and ultimately costs the company more money.

> These shifts in how we think about strategy and planning are important to notice. They expose the fact that for many years and many dollars, we have invested in

planning processes derived from Newtonian beliefs. How many companies made significant gains and consistent progress because of elaborate and costly strategic plans? Very few (Wheatley, 2006, p. 38).

The current educational "system" is clearly a Newtonian structure. By Newtonian, I mean mechanistic. This method of breaking down learning into subjects, age-segregated classrooms, divided physical classrooms, and grading systems perpetuates this antiquated notion of separateness. This reduction into parts and the proliferation of separations has characterized not just organizations, but everything in the Western world during the past three hundred years. We broke knowledge into separate disciplines and subjects, built offices and schools with divided spaces, developed analytical techniques that focus on discrete factors, and even counseled ourselves to act in fragments, to use different "parts" of ourselves in different settings (Wheatley, 2006).

The subtitle of the book, "Education as Enforcement," is "The Corporatization and Militarization of Schooling," and the many critical educators contributing to it make a strong case that education is making the same mistake that corporations have made. The only difference is that the corporations have learned from their mistakes and are now opening to new beliefs in leadership and productivity. Perhaps the model used in these new interwoven corporate leadership styles should be included in the classroom. The students would then be prepared for working in such an environment.

School Reform and Authoritarian Structures

"Authoritarian structures are mechanistic. Power and authority rest almost exclusively in a tightly coupled organization (clear goals and bureaucratic authority guide the organization). Effectiveness is moderate" (Burns, 2003, p. 5). This is the structure found in traditional public schools all over the United States. This structure is counterintuitive to many indigenous cultures' beliefs in leadership and learning. This structure is also heavily utilized in the criminal justice system. The structure within schools prepares the students for the workplace or prison (ACLU, n.d.). Students who do not fare well within the confines of the bureaucratically generated authoritarian structure are often tossed aside into public school "alternative" programs. These programs often tighten the original ineffective controls even further. These alternative programs are not different from their traditional counterparts other than the population in attendance. This population consists of students whom teachers and administrators could no longer handle or teach in the traditional classrooms.

The No Child Left Behind Act of 2001 pressures schools to perform at a certain standard. The students are rigorously tested annually to check for acquired learning. If the students do poorly on these exams, the school is punished, and the federal and state governments remove their financial support. Often, the schools that suffer these consequences are located in the poorest communities. These communities have a higher percentage of second language English learners as well as high criminal activity. Fair Test states:

> Students from low-income and minority-group backgrounds are more likely to be retained in grade, placed in a lower track, or put in special or remedial education

programs when it is not necessary. They are more likely to be given a watered-down or "dummied-down" curriculum, based heavily on rote drill and test practice. This only ensures they will fall further and further behind their peers. On the other hand, children from white, middle and upper income backgrounds are more likely to be placed in "gifted and talented" or college preparatory programs where they are challenged to read, explore, investigate, think and progress rapidly. (Fair Test, 2007, para. 3)

This is another way the current educational system has become a "feeder school" for the criminal system.

School to Prison Pipeline

Criminal activity is often a result of financial instability. Support for poor communities is bleak; adding lack of education to the mix only ensures continued poverty and escalating crime rates. This clearly does not serve the students' best interests. It does, however, look like the functioning of America in the days of slaves. Often the populace of such neighborhoods is made up of the ancestors of those enslaved, the African American. This was intentionally created through districting and house affordability, including access to home loans.

Minorities are often inadvertently forced into the lifestyle of the street due in part by keeping the availability of a high level of education, including an environment conducive to constructive learning, limited or non-existent. This ensures low pay and a life of desperation, a desperation that often leads, again, to criminal activity. Criminal activity leads to prison terms. Prisons utilize these criminals as employees. These employees perform industrial tasks including crop work, license plate manufacturing, among many other "industrial" age type work. These workers can earn anywhere from 8-40 cents per hour. This is clearly an abuse of human life – identical to the use of slave labor.

The school to prison pipeline is well documented (ACLU, n.d.; Fair Test, 2011). Disciplinary actions and various classroom management strategies are often the root of what pushes these children out of the traditional classroom, providing lower literacy rates. Once students find themselves on the street (due to suspension or expulsion), their ensuing lifestyle often lands them in the prison system (National Center for Education Statistics, 1994).

Among adults ages 25 and older, a lower percentage of dropouts are in the labor force compared with adults who earned a high school credential. Among adults in the labor force, a higher percentage of dropouts are unemployed compared with adults who earned a high school credential (U.S. Department of Labor, 2007). Further, dropouts ages 25 or older reported being in worse health than adults who are not dropouts, regardless of income (Pleis and Lethbridge-Çejku, 2006). Dropouts also make up disproportionately higher percentages of the nation's prison and death row inmates (U.S. Department of Education, 2009).

Authoritarian Behavior Observed

Observations I have made in various schools demonstrate how well established this current authoritarian model is. The treatment of public school students is often identical to the treatment of students in juvenile corrections facilities. Observations have included the following:

- Students are required to walk silently in lines with their hands behind their backs. I observed this in Fort Worth Texas, Rancho Mirage California, and Pine Hills Youth Correctional Facility in Miles City Montana.
- Elementary students with desks shoved into corners, backs turned from the rest of the class, excluded due to their behavioral challenges. This can only exacerbate the student's negative self-concept and inadvertently create an autonomous rationality that wants to further rebel against the prevailing "social order." I have personally seen this used in schools in Rosebud and Miles City Montana; Poway, Rancho Mirage, San Jose, Indio, Palm Springs, Desert Hot Springs, Palm Desert, Newark, Temecula, Menifee, La Quinta, and Cathedral City, California; and also in various schools within Spokane, Washington.
- The teacher blows a whistle, all students drop and squat wherever they are, immediately. They stay in this position until they hear the teacher's command. When the teacher blows the whistle again, the students line up. The teachers lead their students to class with their hands behind their backs. This was observed in an elementary school in Rancho Mirage, California.
- Students suspended or expelled for repetitive behavior – not accidentally, right before the standardized testing is to take place. This ensures that this students' scores will not bring down the scores of the whole school and affect the school's funding. I saw this in California.
- Students who pose academic or behavioral problems (often both) are encouraged to be absent the days of the standardized tests. I observed this in California.

• One teacher in National City, CA claimed to me that the teachers at her school give the answers to the students during the standardized test for the school to pass.

Most troubling to me was the use of the whistle conditioning at recess. It is clear that these schools have chosen Pavlovian conditioning (Domjan, 2005) to create a theoretically constructive learning environment. There are teachers who use hand signals and others use different sounds. The effect is the same; the kids develop a learned response for when the teacher signals. Teachers are expected to maintain order (Edwards, 1994). The assumption is that the students are incapable of controlling themselves and thus need an adult to control them (Edwards, 1993). There is no respect for the children's own ability to self-control or self-direct (Edwards, 1989).

School Reform: The Purpose of Education

Before introducing the Indigenous education concepts that contrast authoritarian structures, I want to revisit our Euro-centric education system's purpose. Compulsory education began in America in the 1850's; with the intent to create a society prepared for industrial revolution. Some feel that the industrial revolution created devastation to our natural resources while simultaneously moving our society forward with significant inventions (Hobsbawm, 1999) that have ultimately brought us to the current technological era.

Society has changed tremendously since the initiation of compulsory attendance in public schools. Schools have also changed, but not to the same degree that their world has. The industrial revolution gave way to the technological revolution. Education today focuses on examinations and verification of learning through rote memorization. "Teaching to the test also narrows the curriculum, forcing teachers and students to concentrate on memorization of isolated facts, instead of developing fundamental and higher order abilities" (Fair Test, 2007).

Psychological Development in School

One of the most significant aspects ignored in education is the psychological impact that these reform efforts and authoritarian structures play in brain development. The view of the child as a blank canvas to be painted is antiquated and harmful. The results of this choice can be seen in the society around us. The selfishness and inability to demonstrate emotional intelligence and empathy for others is rampant. The increasing demonstration of narcissistic behavior patterns has been dismissed as generational, yet the very generations making these claims also harbor the same behaviors. The only common theme that all generations have is school.

The efforts made to acknowledge behavior in students was done at the turn of the 20th century and little has been done to question this research. It has been widely accepted and perpetuated for well over a century. With each passing generation, we see ever increasing tendencies toward the disregard of others and the inability to effectively manage healthy boundaries. This has created predatory work environments and has cost worker productivity in many areas of society. In the next chapter, I will discuss narcissism and the role it plays.

~ 4 ~

NARCISSISM

OF ALL OF THE THINGS HUMANKIND CAN SPEND THEIR LIFE ENERGY ON,
NARCISSISM IS THE LARGEST WASTE.
YET ENTIRE GENERATIONS AND SOCIETIES HAVE BEEN
ENSLAVED TO IT FOR CENTURIES....

Narcissism Defined

The American Psychiatric Association defines Narcissistic Personality Disorder in their Diagnostic Manual IV as characterized by a "pervasive pattern of grandiosity, need for admiration, and lack of empathy" (APA, 2013, p. 174). Recent debate by the American Psychiatric Association has been whether it should be continued to be included in further diagnostic manuals due to the pervasiveness of the behaviors within other personality disorders (APA, 2013, p. 67). Another key factor is that narcissism is found in the entire population in varying degrees. It is a fundamental core trait required for survival. The disorder occurs when it is kept at a rudimentary developmental stage.

Narcissism and Evolution

Narcissism is very prevalent throughout history. Although not fully acknowledged in psychology until the later 20th century, it is commonly stated that it is in a minority of the population that struggles with the disorder. However, all persons have some form of narcissism in their functionality. What this really discusses is not that it is a disorder per se. It is more a manifestation of truncated development.

As we have progressed throughout history with our understanding of the world, we see very distinct examples of narcissism gone unchecked. Much of it was widely accepted as the norm and entire nations were run by such structures. Narcissistic hierarchy would be an apt definition. Racism, sexism, adultism, etc. are all manifestations of narcissism gone unchecked. Political structures such as fascism, dictatorships, and similar power indoctrinated leadership are also founded in narcissism. Evolutionary processes would eventually eradicate these truncated developmental delays, but it takes centuries for this type of change to occur. This would also be in direct correlation with the amount of trauma experienced in childhood and adolescence - the time periods with heavy brain development.

Maturation and Narcissism

All children start life with narcissism as it is a core survival trait. Meeting one's needs to survive is essential. Where it goes wrong is when survival is threatened during key developmental periods. Essential needs during these developmental phases include love, physical connection, food, shelter, as well as protection from injury and emotional abuse. Without these key needs being met, the child's brain does not develop beyond the narcissistic state.

During my 26 years of working with children and parenting my own, I have seen direct correlations of behavior patterns between the age groups of 2 and 12 years old. There seems to be a distinct developmental stopping point at both 2 and 12. There is a very logical reason for this as these are two major milestones where a child will begin to assert themselves more confidently in the world.

Many refer to the terrible twos, when really what they are experiencing is agency. At this major developmental milestone, the child is simply realizing they have a desire for things outside of basic survival and dependency. They need more than food, sleep, and safety. They want to explore. They want to do more than they have before. They do not understand danger and they merely want to learn. Parents are frequently exhausted by this constant adventure-oriented behavior. Many become quite aggressive and impatient with their children at this point. This is the point where they start to assert strong disciplinary action to truncate the child's self-determination. This is frequently where many become permanently emotionally developed.

The refusal to allow supported curiosity and reinforcement establishes a craving to meet one's needs however it needs to be done and rebellion is the number one method. The more a parent or caregiver disciplines, the more the child will rebel and protest. Having agency denied is a fundamental development milestone destroyer. The way in which the child is treated during this critical period will mark the future of the child's overall capacity to empathize with others. Inherent selfishness becomes the primary motivation for survival.

I have frequently noted similar behaviors in my middle school grade classrooms. Children at 12 years of age demonstrate the exact same behavior as a two-year-old might, but at this juncture, they have a far larger vocabulary to select from to assert their agency. Many parents relent at the perceived vocal rebellion that initiates at this juncture of development. The common response is to punish and limit with punitive disciplinary action that once again, motivates the child to feel resentment and rebel. Protecting children can be accomplished without such authoritarian action, but the most utilized tactics are those that are aggressive in nature, both verbally and physically. The way in which the children are treated has an impact on the development of their brain at this critical stage of growth. Without proper guidance of their agency, they learn maladaptive reactions rather than learn constructive responses to challenge. When adults utilize such authoritarian mechanisms, they are also demonstrating their own truncated development. They do not have the communication skills to provide adequate response to being challenged, and instead opt for aggression like a toddler's physical and verbal response (yelling, hitting, and threatening). In other words, they never developed skills beyond that first critical agency developmental phase.

How Empires Used Narcissism

This has been practiced for centuries in many cultures. However, not in all cultures. The cultures that were most heavily invested in such a response were those that had a history of predatory behavior designed to conquer other lands and peoples. Cultural cohesion was less important than aiding the Monarchy in achieving its goals. Adhering to this loyalty or threat of death if not adhered to, was the mechanism used by many empires who only viewed their people as pawns to achieve their personal narcissistic goals. Appeasing the masses with promises of protection, land, or other forms of wealth motivated the loyalty. Acknowledgment of what this loyalty truly did to the family was secondary to the promises on offer from the empire.

China was the first to identify the manner in which properly trained government workers could be prepared for this level of loyalty. The Han Dynasty in 500 B.C.E. was the first documented evidence of compulsory schooling in the world's history. What began as preparation for government workers exclusively, later became a means to prepare a workforce for mini-emperors who would employ large numbers of people who needed to be programmed in a manner that would demonstrate obedience, ability to adhere to authority, and loyalty to the state followed by the employer. Family was last on the list of priorities. The family unit needed to be loyal to the state and employer as well.

Due to the trade on the Silk Road between China and Europe, this indoctrination methodology was eventually recognized by Prussia. Prussia was second to instigate compulsory education for their populace. This prepared future soldiers and employees for the Industrial Revolution in the same way that China had identified centuries before.

> The Prussian [education] system [was] designed by Fredrick the Great. King Frederick created a system that was engineered to teach obedience and solidify his control. Focusing on following directions, basic skills, and conformity, he sought to indoctrinate the nation from an early age. Isolating students in rows and teachers in individual classrooms fashioned a strict hierarchy—intentionally fostering fear and loneliness. (The New American Academy, 2018)

What is critical to note is the statement, "intentionally fostering fear and loneliness." This is a key ingredient in narcissistic abuse. I will discuss this later in this chapter. King Frederick ruled Prussia from 1740 to 1786. Under his monarchy, Prussia became one of the greatest states of Europe. His military power was immense.

> He also emerged quickly as a leading exponent of the ideas of enlightened government, which were then becoming influential throughout much of Europe; indeed, his example did much to spread and strengthen those ideas. Notably, his insistence on the primacy of state over personal or dynastic interests and his religious toleration widely affected the dominant intellectual currents of the age (Encyclopedia Britannica Online, 2018, para. 2).

His influence was strong among his contemporaries and his astute focus on fighting any form of "enlightened" thinking influenced monarchies across Europe and Russia. America would follow suit in 1855 with its own compulsory attendance laws. What is critical to note with the timeline and indoctrination of such societal programming, is the order in which communism, fascism, and dictatorships would soon prevail. The murder of the monarchs is what set the tone for societal chaos. The society had been programmed to serve the monarchy. They had no cohesive strategy for self-governance. This made them incredibly vulnerable to predatory despots who saw opportunity to utilize their narcissistic predatory behavior to ensnare entire populations to serve their own megalomaniacal desires.

The situation in America was different. With no monarchy to overthrow, the real challenge was the way in which compulsory education had been enacted a mere 10 years after the abolition of slavery. The country needed a workforce willing to comply with harsh conditions, long hours, and loyalty to the employer. Thus, the growth of unions in the early 20th century. Child labor laws had been enacted to abolish child workers, but then redirect them to schools who would program them to their future employer's desires. Education rarely went past elementary grades, and only those who sought professions in law and medicine went beyond.

This is also when the first wave of feminism began. The right to vote and to be given any voice in the governance of their communities, was especially important to women. They were met with harsh resistance that did not exclude physical violence, imprisonment, and death. Courting was closely monitored by families and marriage was still a financial contract as women were often not able to obtain employment that was not some form of factory work such as seamstresses or cleaning. A rare few owned business or co-ran family owned businesses. Most were dependent upon men for their daily survival. The patriarchal structure was not new, and it also worked well with the narcissistic educational model that made people feel fear and isolation.

Narcissism as a Structure of Control

As previously identified at the start of this chapter, narcissism as a disorder was only recently identified as a problem. The most recent DSM has chosen to remove it as its own disorder since it is so intertwined with many other cluster disorders that promote antisocial behavior. The common behavior in all of them is narcissism. It is also identified by the American Psychiatric Association that every human has a bit of narcissism. The degree to which their expression of it varies. There is, however, a very predictable pattern that can be easily identified in any scenario.

Narcissistic abuse consists of three components. Those components are the narcissist/predator, their chosen victim(s), and the "flying-monkeys" rallied by the narcissist to reinforce their efforts and do their bidding. Very frequently, the narcissist will utilize the flying monkeys to abuse for them. This can be very clearly seen in the previously mentioned empires, especially when the monarchies fell and were replaced by dictators. The dictators themselves did not commit the crimes. They would rally the population to do it for them.

As identified previously, fear and isolation are key ingredients. The three primary goals of any narcissistic abuse pattern are: Fear, Obligation, and Guilt (FOG). There are also very predictable behavior patterns utilized to reinforce FOG. They are as follows:

Narcissistic abusers never apologize. They always believe themselves to be above any potential wrong and as such deem themselves right. If they do apologize, it is disingenuous and only serves to support convincing the receiver of the apology to give the narcissist what they want. However, they feel that they are the victims of their own wrongdoing. The way in which they re-frame and project their own behavior onto others confuses the listener so that the listener at some point may feel at fault for what the narcissist did.

They believe themselves to be above reproach. Their perfectionistic self-ideal prevents them from acknowledging their mistakes or in taking responsibility for their actions. At this point, they project their mistakes onto others, who will likely be willing to take responsibility if the victimized position of the narcissist is worded convincingly enough.

They are incapable of self-reflection and self-analysis. Lack of self-awareness is a hallmark of narcissistic personalities. They hold an objective incapacitation that cannot be rectified by thoughtful communicative discourse. They do not reflect on their beliefs or their actions. Their impulsive behavior demonstrates their lack of analytical reasoning and their behavior demonstrates a determination to fulfill their instant gratification over the well-being of those who may be impacted by such actions.

Inability to forgive. In addition to never apologizing, they also do not accept apologies. Their belief that they are entitled to whatever they wish, due to their perfect self-perception. They expect others to meet their every demand. Anything less is intolerable. They do not forget, and they are revengeful.

Their behavior is never selfless or thoughtful. Any notions of "generosity" come with an expectation of getting something they want. Generosity is not actual generosity. It is an unspoken acknowledgment of a debt to be repaid at will in the way the narcissist deems qualified to "repay" their "generosity." Acceptance of "gifts" is really acceptance of debt.

They never reveal their real emotions. They like to be the center of attention and relish the spotlight. They will put on a show to maintain this attention. It does not matter if the attention is negative or positive. They are emotionally closed off to others. This is a protective mechanism developed early in life to protect them from something. This likely could stem from their first attempts at agency around the age of two years old.

They are insensitive and not able to empathize with others. Due to their own inability to understand their own feelings, they are unable to understand the feelings of others. Insensitivity and tactlessness are frequent markers to note. Words they speak are provided without consideration of the impact on the audience who receives it. They are often perceived as reliable sources due to their lack of emotional connectivity to what they say. They know how to generate a reaction from others due to years of attempts to feel emotion. By creating emotional reactions in others, they get to experience these emotions. The only emotion they are truly in touch with is anger. Again, a direct result from their first attempts at agency. They experienced anger and they were the recipients of anger. This became an indoctrinated understanding early on. Through their charismatic speeches designed to provoke emotional reactions, they can manipulate others to follow them and trust them, despite the evidence that their words are false. This falls under the conditioning of flying monkeys and victims of narcissists who are programmed young to survive narcissistic abuse by choosing enabling behaviors (fawning) to protect themselves from the abuse.

Flying monkeys (enablers) and scapegoats (victims)

As mentioned previously, the enablers of the narcissist's actions are the primary producers of the abuse done to victims. If a narcissist is approached by the victim and called into account for their actions, the enablers will defend the narcissist for fear of falling out of favor with the narcissist and facing retribution for not demonstrating loyalty. The way that a narcissist garners their loyalty is through promises, special acknowledgment, or privilege for doing as the narcissist requests. They are given "rewards" for going against their own beliefs and demonstrating loyalty to the narcissist. They are effectively handing over their agency to the narcissist when they participate in this exchange. When later called into account for their actions, they frequently use words such as, "it was my job," or "I didn't think I had a choice." In some cases, they could have been threatened for not doing what was requested of them. A form of coercion or duress is enacted to force compliance. They are not allowed to question the validity or integrity of the instructions or the person giving them. Challenging the narcissist is not just discouraged, it is met with vehement aggression, threats, and threat of abandonment by the narcissist. Other threats include destruction of reputation, financial survival, or approval by the narcissist. The loyalty is only fully achieved after a lengthy grooming period of abundant attention, praise, and privilege. It is at this juncture where requests that go against the enabler's own integrity will be requested of them. They have been chosen because they are special.

The scapegoat is the target of the narcissist's abuse. The one they want to weaken, destroy, or control. The scapegoat is often identified as a threat to the narcissist. They demonstrate a strength that triggers insecurity in the narcissist. This strength can range from intelligence, physical appearance, privilege, success, financial prowess, and many other factors that trigger jealousy. The scapegoat may not even be aware that the narcissist even notices them. They may believe they are nothing special and do not even see the things that the narcissist is jealous of. They are frequently minding their own business, and the narcissist will insert him or herself into the victim's life to begin their grooming process to gain loyalty of the scapegoat. It is no different than the enabler grooming period. The difference between the two is that the scapegoat will not demonstrate loyalty. Their integrity is stronger, and they are much less likely to stand by and watch something happen to someone without speaking out. The narcissist may even begin destroying the life of the scapegoat long before they are threatened publicly by the scapegoat. They wish to weaken this "threat" before it has an opportunity to outshine or call out the narcissist's behavior. So, they may systematically put things in place to ruin the scapegoat's life yet do it in a way that makes them look like they are supporting and helping the scapegoat. This is when the flying monkeys are used to perform the actions that the narcissist does not want affiliated with them. After all, trust cannot be gained if they are caught in the act. The goal of the narcissist is to remove this threat and to keep them down so that they do not get in the way of the narcissist's goals.

The following chapter will discuss how narcissism is programmed into populations and the effects it has on education and the way in which society functions.

~ 5 ~

THE RESULTS OF PROGRAMMED
NARCISSISM

The fall of the Kingdoms perpetuated the dictatorships in Europe and Asia. The countries that did not befall communist dictators were those where the monarchy was willing to allow a democratic government. Those monarchs were not murdered.

America never had a monarchy. Schools were enacted and fully reinforced in the 1800's and early 1900's. Students were not being trained to serve a monarch. They did not befall a dictatorship because there was no monarch to murder. However, they were programmed to create a unified nation and workforce through their schools.

America was ahead of programming the masses to eradicate individual cultural norms, rituals, and beliefs. Dictators took swaths of countries and tried to formulate nationalist rhetoric to unify the people. These failed significantly in areas where there were too many different cultures. These cultures often fought the forced erasure of their identity. America has yet to accomplish this goal. Even now we still see education attempting to eradicate history, to erase cultural understanding, and to discourage diverse languages. This forced limitation was designed to create a cohesive culture, yet more than 160 years of compulsory education has yet to achieve this in America.

So why did it even survive this long in America? Well, the dictatorships were implemented on lands where the people had always been. There was a sense of place and ownership over the land. Their ancestors were buried there. They had a history that was thousands of centuries old. Abuse was the only method which was consistently utilized across all dictatorships to reinforce compliance with removal of one's need to hold on to identity.

In America, the only people who had the same struggle were the Native Americans. African Americans were not in America by choice. The rest were immigrants looking for opportunity or fleeing tyranny at home. They had no "place" anymore and they were more willing to succumb to an external party telling them who they needed to be to stay there. Yet, the people deciding the narrative were not the ones who had a true historic belonging to this land. Only the Native Americans did. So, the genocide of the Native American population and harsh stripping of their cultural identity was acutely focused on. This later led to widespread alcoholism, abuse, and severe poverty in their individual tribal nations. All colonization across the globe used religious programming to reinforce subservient behavior. This was the closest thing to a Kingdom that America had known.

European settlers had already been subjected to Kingdoms and the partnership with the Church. they did not question it. Some came to America to explore religious freedom, some of which was worse than the religions enforced in their homelands. Others found a more compassionate strategy, yet it was still a forced indoctrination reinforced by external parties and a deity (King). "Free will" was given lip service, but vehemently punishable, even by death.

The use of the term "free will" has been advocated throughout the centuries to give the people a semblance of choice and to make them feel that they have control over their reality. Yet, stories tell how failure to do as one is told will lead to poverty, abuse, sexual abuse, imprisonment, or death. Sometimes all of these. The purveyors of moral code were some of the most abusive people around. In fact, they are quite the opposite of what they preach. Their predatory behavior also had nothing to do with wealth or one's station in life. Anyone could snatch the reins of power by proclaiming religious superiority.

Programmed Narcissism

Stanley Milgram performed an experiment that was published in 1973 relating to what lengths people will go in order to follow authority. He found that people were more willing to harm others if ordered to than they were to defy authority (Milgram, 1973). He believed that obedience is deeply ingrained in the social order. All social orders require someone in authority, people who submit to the authority, and people who defy authority (Milgram, 1973). He also states that these factors surpass any "training in ethics, sympathy, or moral conduct" (Milgram, 1973, p. 62).

What his experiment does not consider is the possibility that society has been programmed to obey authority and this programming runs deeper than any education relating to defiance of authority for the sake of morality or ethics. Fear has much to do with this.

This begins with parenting. Children who are raised in a home where punishments that resulted in isolation and exclusion train the children that they are not worthy and will not be included unless they comply. This generates a conditioned loneliness. Loneliness increases neurological self-preservation behaviors. So, parents or others who treat a child in a manner such as time-out, sending them to their room and forcibly denying them connection, isolating them in the classroom, or excluding them from family or school outings reinforces narcissistic self-preservation behaviors. These behaviors include hypervigilance, lack of empathy, and more. Adults are given free rein to violate a child's boundaries and autonomy, which then begins the development of narcissistic abuse training and conditioning.

Loneliness increases morning cortisol levels, the stress hormone (Cacioppo, 2013). It creates a hypervigilance setting the brain to look for potential threats (Cacioppo, 2013). This makes the brain see threats where they may or may not exist (Cacioppo, 2013). This also creates memory biases regarding social interactions (Cacioppo, 2013). All of which increases the likelihood of increased negative interactions with others (Cacioppo, 2013). It increases defensiveness because the person who feels lonely is only focused on how they feel and not how others feel (Cacioppo, 2013). Loneliness increases prepotent responding, which means that impulsive behaviors will increase (Cacioppo, 2013). It also disturbs sleep cycles because the brain is still in hypervigilance mode to self-protect (Cacioppo, 2013). Symptoms of what many label as Attention Deficit Hyperactivity Disorder are very likely symptoms of severe loneliness and not receiving adequate nor appropriate attention. The way in which adults treat children exacerbates the very issue the child is already reacting from and it becomes a downward spiral that goes out of control without someone to stop the cycle.

If we were to label this as a mental disorder, we would be dismissing the fact that it is a physical developmental disorder. It was created by the society in which the child grew up and as such, the society is responsible for the creation of what results. A two-year-old child is not going to be forced to think unequivocally the same way a 42-year-old would. Psychologically, two-year-old children are incapable of understanding at that level. If only certain portions of the brain were affected, one could easily have the brain of a 42-year-old with limitations in the prefrontal cortex as a direct result of childhood traumas impacting brain development. Thus the 42-year-old's ability to make rational decisions, regulate emotions, and think beyond the way a self-serving two-year-old can would not be absurd.

The challenge lies in the fact that one cannot control all adult interaction situations or experiences that a child might have to prevent the trauma that truncates development. However, we can make strides as a society to stop the current socially acceptable behaviors that are very clearly developmentally inappropriate and abusively reinforced. Physical punishment, as well as psychological manipulation of children, are two major components we need to address. Narcissistic behaviors are often transferred within family lines just as abuse cycles run in families. It can be broken, but it takes a lot of education and retraining people on how to interact with children when working with those in traumatic situations or who have gone through traumatic situations.

Unfortunately, we also find predatory people in the "helping" fields such as social services, psychology, and education. These predators vary from those who seek to violate a child in seriously inappropriate manners, but also those who seek to manipulate children as if they were puppets. Those who use children as a way to live out their own deeper desires or dreams (overzealous parents or coaches who want the child to be a superstar). We also see it in people who are desperate to find something wrong with the child and proceed to demand focus on how overwhelmed they are with the child and that they don't understand why the child has so many problems (often a direct result of schools or daycares not having the capacity to actually work appropriately with a child to meet the child's actual needs). Some parents utilize the carrot on a stick manipulation method that is reinforced by the schools who encourage parents to do these things in the home environment. The schools will not take responsibility for their contribution to the child's behavior. They are always quick to blame the parent(s). Neither parents nor schools are listening to the child.

The rare few who do not reinforce the procession ensuring adult needs are always met, without consideration of the child's needs, are frequently attacked. The children have no escape. They are at the mercy of adults who spend their time policing the behavior of other adults to ensure the result is attention on the adults and convenience for the adults. The child is just the product the adults deal with. It's all about the adults. If this is what a child grows up with, then we cannot expect them to grow up to be a well-adjusted and productive member of society when all of the adults in the child's life went out of their way to ensure the child was kept in a state of unacceptable, a problem, needing help, and perpetually never good enough or of value. They were just a pawn in a grown-up game of "look at me!" They learn narcissism from the adults who raised them. They learn that what is morally and ethically sound is not important. They learn that doing what you are told surpasses any personal feelings or concerns.

Drugging children for the schools is something the pharmaceutical industry, medical, and psychiatric industry joined forces with the education field to generate more jobs for adults using the children as fodder for their needs to be met. If a child has attention-deficit, it means they are not getting enough attention. Yet the solution we see is to drug them, rather than to change the adults in the equation and how they respond to the child.

Adults will never admit to being the reason that children are behaving badly. Children are like frogs in the pond. They start developing odd legs and such when chemical spills happen in their environment. They try to draw your attention to it but are almost always dismissed or misunderstood because adults only see things from their own perspective. They very infrequently attempt to understand what the child might be thinking or experiencing, or they do not have the capacity to interpret or understand. Rather than seeking help to ask what the child is saying, they seek help to find a way to control the child. Thus, perpetuating and exacerbating the problem.

When the abused become the abusers they are no better, but often far worse than the monster they were trying to defeat. Their numbers can destroy entire nations and populations with contempt and murderous retaliation. Facts do not matter because their cognitive dissonance will not allow anything to redirect their narcissistic rage.

The human mind can be easily manipulated if people set in place the right programmatic materials for consumption. The reason gun control is not taken seriously in America is because society is easy to manipulate due to the programming. If propaganda is spread to bring narcissistic rage, people will willingly use those weapons to harm citizens without remorse. I have seen how oppressed members of society start behaving in the same manner as their abuser(s) to feel safe and theoretically heard. All this does is increase the abuse in society. It is not justice. It does not create the equality that they seek. It creates equality of abuse only. This response is then used to reinforce how dangerous they were to begin with, which only reinforces their oppression.

I find it fascinating when people think themselves impervious to dictatorship or similar situations that have occurred in other nations. They think themselves superior and more intelligent. They are literally stating that all other countries who have befallen to such leadership were ignorant and stupid. Now, what that really is, is heavily misguided narcissism and cognitive dissonance reinforcing their self-belief to being above reproach. There is no more dangerous position than to be like this. In fact, it is this level of self-identification that generated the dictatorships that resulted. Severe national pride and belief in superiority.

Children vs. Adults

Adults expect coddling or aggression as the only two forms of communicating with children. They were likely yelled at or praised for everything as a child, so they only know aggression or coddling as an adult. They were never spoken to as logical intelligent beings as children, so when they are spoken to like this as an adult, they think they are being insulted if they don't know something. There is an inherent need to be superior, which makes sense since compulsory education taught them that you mean nothing unless you compete and are on top. So those who suddenly no longer feel they are on top become contemptuous. They even feel that their own limited knowledge and experience trumps those who are career researchers and experts in the field. This is all cognitive dissonance.

All of this was highly developed in schools. Parents merely reinforce school demands since parents are beholden to schools. People literally advise others to appease narcissistic abuse out of professional protocol. One can be considered unprofessional for expecting intellectual discourse to be allowed conversation. Do not expect respectful treatment or one can be deemed as wrong simply for speaking up and even addressing another as an equal or someone who should respect anyone else.

Personal Experience

I taught students by helping them teach each other and giving them ownership over their experience and speaking with them in a manner that encouraged self-reflection and opportunity for change. Adults don't like that very much. They get angry and offended when you do that with them. Adults were raised with teachers that controlled them, told them what to do, gave them gold stars, and punished or shamed them. So, their perception of the world was shaped by this treatment. When you hold a mirror up and discuss behavior, they take it as a personal attack.

When speaking with a child about their behavior, be sure to separate the behavior from the person. Be sure they understand that. They are not the behavior. They can control the behavior. They cannot control "who" they are. When you make them feel like the "who" is being attacked, they get on the defensive and narcissistic rage is unleashed. What I am noticing with adults is their cognitive dissonance over new information sets them into hypervigilance, projections, gaslighting, and narcissistic rage. They take literally everything as a personal attack on their character. That is because they were raised that way. So, to talk to adults, there is a level of unprogramming them that has to happen in order to get them to the point of hearing what is being said. If they are coddled through that process, they won't hear what is being said. They are only seeking the comfort that comes from relieving the cognitive dissonance. This means their belief won't change because it is back to what they know.

The education system and authoritarian parenting paradigm has literally created an entire adult populace that cannot handle looking at their own behaviors and self-reflecting. Nor do they know how to find information to change. They rely upon others to tell them everything. They seek constant validation for everything they do and become angry when they are ignored or given feedback that would help them improve.

Adults avoid being honest with each other and often choose passive-aggressive behavior to avoid being responsible for their actions. They fear speaking honestly and they feel like they have to either avoid the person expecting honesty (perhaps to deal with their own issues or because they don't know how to respond because they feel challenged), act dramatically, go to their room, and slam the door, or they act like nothing happened and avoid the topic completely. Resolution is never found through any of these methods. The only thing that happens through this behavior is the festering of the wound, which will only get worse.

Adults cannot cope. They have learned narcissistic abuse either by becoming abusive or by responding to being controlled by a narcissist. Examples include:

- Women advising other women to be wary of men.
- Co-workers advise each other to remain silent and take the clearly abusive situation at work to keep their jobs.
- People advising others to appease the abuser (parent/spouse/even child sometimes) to keep the family together because the image of family is more important than psychological well-being.
- Everyone was trained to shut-up and take it.

- When confronted over the actual behavior, the abuse commences.
- The cognitive dissonance goes into overdrive.
- The narcissistic rage becomes the central focus

Hypervigilance is a programmed response to trauma. There is a lot of hysteria in American television and news. The media is constantly pumping narcissism to the masses, normalizing it so that people don't question the behaviors and the society they find themselves in. They may stand dumbfounded and surprised by the way the world seems to be, but they will never question what their accepted systems have done to contribute to this. They will not question their own parenting that is considered the norm. They believe they are doing right. They are doing their best. They are doing what they know. What they know is being reinforced by external parties that keep the entire society in hypervigilance. Hypervigilance makes the population easier to manipulate.

Abusers keep their victims on edge. They keep their victims feeling insecure. They keep their victims fearing. They use dramatic loud sounds to reinforce this fear. Shock value to numb the senses so they can make people dissociate and be easier to control. Exposure to healthy human behavior is uncommon because conditioning from intentionally hysterical behavior makes populations easier to control.

Narcissism and Basic Survival

When comparing humanity with the natural world, we tend to separate ourselves by our ability to be creative, artistic, produce architectural wonders, and many more amazing things that cannot be done by any other species on the planet. We also associate this with having the ability to have empathy, sympathize, and show an array of emotions not frequently identified in the wild. This does not mean that these emotions or abilities do not exist in the wild. It suggests that humanity has not yet been able to fully understand the creatures in the wild, despite their determination to understand and conquer nature. One factor that humanity holds in equity with wild animals is narcissism.

SURVIVAL OF THE FITTEST

We have all heard people preach their strong positions by using terms such as survival of the fittest, only the strong survive, and many others. Some even use these phrases to justify doing heinous acts to those they deem weaker or less than. The means by which humanity has taken this instinct has gone far more insidiously than any wild creature has ever fathomed.

Fear is a mighty motivator. Fear of loss of control. Just as it is easier to control victims by reinforcing narcissistic behaviors to constantly move the goal-posts, gaslight them, project on them, and isolate them with silence so they always question themselves, thus preventing them from standing up and doing something - those victims do the same to other groups who are in positions weaker than their own. Removing support of identity, support of self-awareness, support of improving core identity with confidence, is not a mistake. It is intentional. It is narcissism.

Narcissism is Fear of Death

Narcissism is a core human survival mechanism. Those who have learned how to navigate the world either improve their strategies (especially if given healthy mentorship and guidance), or they remain stuck because the world has hardened them and they cannot let that guard down for one second for fear of death. That is what it really is. It is fear of death.

Narcissism is fear. It is fear of death. Death of the ego, but more importantly death of the familiar. The unknown is what terrifies because it cannot be controlled. So, something one cannot control feels like death. It is fear of death. Man's fear of nature is exactly this. The need to control it to ensure survival. Unfortunately, man can never truly control nature, for in the attempt to control nature, he kills himself.

Teaching Narcissism in Schools

Schools aren't about the kids. It is all about the adults and what they are getting out of it. The education industry in America is one of the largest employers and the most guaranteed supply of job security due to the focus of its product. It is unfortunate to reduce it to such factors, but when attempts to focus on the children and the psychological impact made on them, priorities become clear. It does not lie with the children and their highest development. It is about efficient processing of products for funding guarantee and job security. Others also look at it as childcare. The testing machine is also about jobs and product manufacture. The sheer depth of how far the educational job creation front covers is far and wide. It includes every single facet of manufacture imaginable. It also separates the children from the real world.

The separation of school from life sets people up to separate navigating the world and communicating with others in a constructive manner. It turns into a free-for-all dominance competition. Rather than serving as each other's teachers and students, we turn into people who feel we must prove we're right over literally anyone else and then people feel attacked if they are corrected. Now the way one is corrected is part of the issue. Most people assert their "knowledge" in a form of dominance over the other, thus the crumbling of any constructive debate or mutual navigation of the topic.

Imagine how different our political landscape would be if we were to suddenly start communicating in a more receptive fashion. The largest factor to note is that the dominating behavior is reactionary. It is not responsive. Reaction is a means for manipulation and directing people to lose their self-control. This makes them easier to control. When they are out of control, you can sell them anything or get them to react any way you want them to because they are easy to make emotional/volatile/lacking in self-control.

This is done intentionally. If you want a healthy country, you have to start by communicating like the perfect classroom environment where the teacher speaks to students from a position of understanding them and not speaking condescendingly while they restate how students see the situation and offer other alternatives for students to consider. The challenge with this is that it requires people to be patient with one another. It requires time.

When I tried to introduce this to public school teachers through means of introducing democracy for classroom management, their #1 response was, "we don't have time for that." Think about that for a minute.

Empathy

A recent study involving 11 experiments and 1,200 participants resulted in demonstrating that people would not choose empathy regardless of positive feelings due to the amount of effort involved

(Cameron et al., 2019). The researchers did find that if participants were told they were more empathetic than the other group, they would be more likely to choose things that demonstrated more empathy (Cameron et al., 2019). This further reinforces the way education has programmed them to respond to what they are told, as in being told who or what they are and living up to that. This is an approval seeking behavior and is demonstrated in all narcissistic power dynamic relationships. Participants saw the researchers as the experts and more knowledgeable, so when told by these researchers that they were more empathetic, they believed it and did it. However, when left on their own or told that they weren't as empathetic as the other group, they did not choose empathetic options.

This further reinforces what Milgram suggested. That participants will obey authority without thinking. If they are told to harm someone, they are more likely to follow orders. If they are told they are more empathetic, they will prove they are more empathetic. They are not taking independent moral or ethical stands based upon their own beliefs. They take their own self-beliefs from external sources first. In fact, the researchers also found that most of the participants had a very strong preference to avoid showing empathy even when the example was expressing joy (Cameron et. al, 2019). Researchers believed it had to do with the participants considering it to be more effort to choose empathy (Cameron et. al, 2019).

A recent study from the University of California Berkeley found that various studies spanning over twenty years demonstrated that those who were in a position of power demonstrated behaviors reminiscent of those who have suffered traumatic brain injuries (Keltner, 2016). They behaved more impulsively, were less aware of the risks they were taking, and were challenged in empathizing with others (Keltner, 2016). Naish and Obhi (2015) also found that when in positions responding to power, participants were able to mirror the responses of the person of authority. However, when participants were the person of authority, they were unable to mirror the responses of those in positions below them. This lack of mirroring or responsive empathy was reinforced through Transcranial Magnetic Stimulation.

Keltner studies behaviors and the research of Naish and Obhi studies the brain itself. Both studies demonstrated a lack of empathy and ability to relate to others for those who wield some sort of power. Effort to produce empathy did not change the results. Neurologists, Lord David Owen and Jonathan Davidson, define this as Hubris syndrome, "a disorder of the possession of power, particularly power which has been associated with overwhelming success, held for a period of years, and with minimal constraint on the leader" (Owen & Davidson, 2009, p.1397).

Licensed psychotherapist, Bree Bonchay, LCSW has purported that over 158 million people in the United States are affected by narcissistic abuse (Bonchay, 2018). "There are 304 million persons in the U.S. One in 25 people will have the disorders associated with 'no conscience' which include antisocial personality disorder, sociopath, and psychopath. Three hundred and four million divided by 25 = 12.16 million people with no conscience" (Brown, 2010, para. 4-5).

The damage goes beyond the personal impact to the individual. Everyone impacted by narcissistic abuse impacts our medical systems, work environments, school systems, and social environments. This increased stress response impacts people with physical and psychological symptoms. Symptoms vary from person to person, but can include heart attack, weight gain or loss, anxiety, depression, Post Traumatic Stress Syndrome, insomnia, autoimmune disorders, migraines, epilepsy, digestion issues, arthritis, cancer, Type 2 Diabetes, alcohol and drug addiction, high cholesterol, and much more. One would normally consider these negative problems for a society to bear, but when you look at the economic results, this generates numerous jobs. More things to sell. More people to medicate. More patients to treat. There is no motivation to stop this problem. It is a huge money-maker.

~ 6 ~

TRAUMA AND BRAIN
DEVELOPMENT

Introduction

There are two distinct ages when the brain is vulnerable to trauma due to high neurological development. Researcher, Jay Geidd, M.d., has found that up until the age of 5 to 6 years old, children develop 95% of the structure of their brain (2014). A secondary phase of development occurs in the prefrontal cortex around 11 to 12 years, just before puberty (Geid, 2014). These are the two phases when children find themselves facing the reactions adults have to their newly inspired independence.

Toddlers suddenly want to explore independently of their parents, and are frequently told no, put in the corner (separation from love or nurture), spanked, or put in some form of limiting situation. Outside of any opinion relating to the methods used by the parent or caregiver, the experience the child has is restriction of their independence followed by some form of trauma to reinforce this. This becomes a fixed pain memory.

It can also inhibit the growth and development of the brain. This was found to be especially true in a study done with Romanian orphans after the fall of communist Romania. Babies were not held due to fear of germs; however, they were provided all necessities. It was found that the babies who were not held grew up to become adults with mental health issues and found functioning in the adult world difficult (Hamilton, 2014). It has been found that lack of physical connection, loving interactions, affection, and closeness decreases brain development, which later results in mental health issues (Hamilton, 2014). One could easily argue that physical abuse, such as spanking, slapping, or any kind of physical aggression intended as discipline can be received by the child's developing brain as trauma.

Carrion and colleagues (2009) found that children who experience emotional distress at a young age have higher incidence of cortisol, a stress hormone, and decreased hippocampus size. Children with these symptoms also demonstrated emotional challenges and difficulties with memory recall. Treadway and colleagues (2019) identified how certain people are more sensitive to inflammation impacting the brain resulting in lack of motivation. Since there is no way to know which children will be predisposed to inflammation, as a result of trauma, impacting their brain development and how it results in dispositions such as depression, schizophrenia, or other impairments, it is worth considering that the way children are treated should be given more consideration with regard to the trauma they are being required to endure under the guise of discipline.

Evolutionary Purpose

Since Darwin's scientific position on evolution, there has been much research on human development. One psychiatrist, Randolph Nesse, is one of the founders of evolutionary medicine. He has written that natural selection does not remove psychiatric disorders from human evolution for a reason. 20% of Americans are currently suffering from some sort of mental illness and nearly 50% will experience mental illness at one or more periods in their lifetime. Dr. Nesse, attributes this to our genes being impacted by our surroundings with little regard to our current scenario (Nesse, 2019). One could label this as part of epigenetic programming. Another might say that this is programmed trauma conditioning. Both are likely correct and work in tandem.

Our responses may very well be epigenetic memory from experiences that our ancestors had. So, this also offers the potential for epigenetic trauma memory to be passed down to future generations to ensure survival of the species. I will discuss epigenetics in much more detail in chapter six. What makes this challenging for those treating people who demonstrate mental illness, is identifying if this is in response to a current trauma, an inherited trauma, or pathological. Better yet, is the pathological issue really an inherited trauma? Although I would not dismiss pathology having a much wider influence on brain functionality and neurological processes, epigenetics are definitely a wild card that is harder to manage as a therapist than something that can be worked through as a current trauma or a pathological malfunction due to biological issues.

Development

Evolution applies to all species, not just humanity. It has also been found that lack of self-control in adolescence is also not unique to humanity. Primates and humans alike appear to go through the same neurological developmental phases (Constantinidis & Luna, 2019).

> As is widely known, adolescence is a time of heightened impulsivity and sensation-seeking, leading to questionable choices. However, this behavioral tendency is based on an adaptive neurobiological process that is crucial for molding the brain based on gaining new experiences...They have a developed prefrontal cortex and follow a similar trajectory with the same patterns of maturation between adolescence and adulthood. (Luna, 2019, pp.604-605)

This developmental phase provides key information about the environment in order for the primate or human to develop more specialized facets in the brain (Constantinidis & Luna, 2019). This is a key developmental factor tied to cognitive maturation (Constantinidis & Luna, 2019). As a result of this tendency toward impulsivity and the responses from the adults, the developing mind learns to navigate the obstacles and risks.

It is easy to understand that if an adult aggressively responds to the adolescent, they learn that the adult is a threat. This will further program their mind to learn to do what they want to do without being noticed by the adult to avoid the adult's response. This is why in traditionally raised households, we see children rebelling and sneaking around, especially in their teen years. Instead of learning survival skills that would be the goal of the adults, the teen learns to avoid authority to not experience the same reaction again.

The same can also be found in nations with former dictatorships. It is incredibly difficult to take a programmed society and expect them to understand democracy or how to behave in a manner that is collaborative if there is anyone in the society who implements any form of limitation or control. This has been especially obvious in our most recent COVID-19 pandemic. Observing behaviors across nations has been interesting. Those with former dictatorships tend to behave in manners like sneaky teenage behavior. Those who were used to oppressing other groups are rebelling dramatically against being controlled themselves. Those in societies that have been more universally supportive (socialist in nature) have been much less resistant, and thus needed fewer external controls implemented. Those in current dictatorships were already used to knowing they had to follow the rules or experience potentially lethal consequences. Rebellion isn't really an option for them. This type of leadership takes immense levels of abusive threats to continuously implement and it creates a society that will never know how to behave when they are in other countries that do not operate this way. When they are in another country, they tend to misbehave more because they have no idea how to handle freedom.

Frequent strategies to motivate "good" behavior are what has been commonly known as award system training. This goes back to the previously mentioned operant conditioning identified by B.F. Skinner. Recent research has utilized artificial intelligence to identify that the dopamine system operates by training the prefrontal cortex "to operate as its own free-standing learning system" (Wang et al., 2018, p. 860). This may support other learning, but it is important to note how it is a completely different learning system and the portion of the brain targeted by this type of training is directly involved in the same portion of the brain responsible for impulsivity and risk. This actually poses concern since what this would suggest is that training the area of the brain that is responsible for risk taking and impulsivity is being trained without awareness of how that impacts the overall intellectual capacity of the individual. It has no bearing on the individual learning any material other than behavioral award. It also programs this portion of the brain to avoid negative consequences, which then promotes behavior that will navigate around the controls which inhibit direct participation. For some individuals, this will help them to know to not do certain things when certain people are around, but it by no means teaches them to not do these things when authority is absent. Self-control is never developed.

> Strong evidence indicates that reciprocal connections between the amygdala and the medial prefrontal cortex (mPFC) support fundamental aspects of emotional behavior in adulthood. However, this circuitry is slow to develop in humans, exhibiting immaturity in childhood. The argument is made that the development of this circuitry in humans is intimately associated with caregiving, such that parental availability during childhood provides important and enduring scaffolding of neuroaffective processes that ultimately form of the nature of the adult phenotype. (Tottenham, 2015, p. 489)

This could also feed into the issues that appear to be so common in American classrooms. In the last two decades the numbers of children diagnosed with attention deficit disorder has skyrocketed. The same can be said for autism and diagnoses associated with behavioral issues. With the type of caregiving provided to children in America, it is concerning to see these numbers increase so dramatically. If these were truly biologically detrimental issues, then treatment would be warranted. However, it would appear that the increased pressure schools have to demand performance from students through standardized examinations and increasing traumatic experiences on campus and off, it would be more appropriate to question the environment we are subjecting the children to rather than masking their symptoms with medication so that we continue business as usual.

Case Western Reserve University School of Medicine has discovered that various psychiatric disorders such as bipolar disorder, schizophrenia, major depression, and various other attention disorders display an inability for two different brain regions to communicate. They attribute it to the ERbB4 gene,a receptor of neuregulin-1. "Our findings give importance to synchrony between the prefrontal cortex and hippocampus in top-down attention and open up the possibility that attention deficit disorders, like ADHD, might involve impairments in the synchrony between these two regions" (Mei et al., 2018, p. 391). It is important to acknowledge the gene impact of this as it is also something that could very easily be implicated in epigenetic memory, as will be discussed in chapter six.

Dopamine is also a factor that up until now, has not been considered deeply important in the learning process. Wang and colleagues have identified that dopamine plays an integral role in the meta-learning process (2016). Their research has identified that dopamine not only strengthens synaptic links in the prefrontal cortex system, which reinforces behavior, but it also transmits and embeds important details about abstract tasks and rule structures in order to adapt to new tasks easily (Wang et al., 2016). The dopamine is what produces this transfer of information which provides versatility not found in the synapse structures alone (Wang et al., 2016).

> Dopamine is an important endogenous catecholamine which exerts widespread effects both in neuronal (as a neurotransmitter) and non-neuronal tissues (as an autocrine or paracrine agent). Within the central nervous system, dopamine binds to specific membrane receptors presented by neurons and it plays the key role in the

control of locomotion, learning, working memory, cognition, and emotion. The brain dopamine system is involved in various neurological and psychiatric disturbances such as Parkinson's Disease, schizophrenia, and amphetamine and cocaine addiction. (Drozak & Bryla, 2005, p. 405.

What this signifies is the implication of how the learning experience can impact the processing of information through the dopamine system.

Childhood trauma is a risk factor for psychosis. Amphetamine increases synaptic striatal dopamine levels and can induce positive psychotic symptoms in healthy individuals and patients with schizophrenia. Socio-developmental hypotheses of psychosis propose that childhood trauma and other environmental risk factors sensitize the dopamine system to increase the risk of psychotic symptoms, but this remains to be tested in humans. (Dahoun et al., 2019 p. 1)

In addition to the potential for psychological dysregulation as a result of traumatic learning experiences, it has also been found to impact the ability to empathize with others, which is a common issue found in those who have been diagnosed with various attention deficit disorders. One area of study that has been integral in understanding how the brain learns is the study of music. This research has been found to demonstrate increased neurotransmitter development in those who have studied music versus those who have not. (Gangrade, 2012). Increased neurotransmitter development improves connectivity between different regions of the brain and accelerates learning (Gangrade, 2012). Additionally, researchers have identified how those who demonstrate higher levels of empathy tend to choose pro-social decision-making when observing others and this can be observed through MRI scans in mirror regions of the brain (Christov-Moore and Iacoboni, 2016; Christov-Moore et al., 2017b).

It would be very likely that without the additional support of music education, the traumas experienced in the learning environment, home environment, or society would create irreconcilable shortages in brain development for many students who would then fail to empathize with others and be productive members of society. This is not to say that music education should replace a healthy learning and home environments. It should be used in addition to these. It is not a band-aid. To assume as much would be to gravely misunderstand the importance of healthy environment creation. However, for students who were experiencing grave trauma, music has often been a major salvation not only for their intellectual development, but also as a trauma coping mechanism.

Trauma's Influence on Brain Development

Stress impacts our daily lives. It has repercussions that can influence our overall physical and psychological health. Research into how stress impacts the brain and brain development has shed light on how seriously we need to consider its impact on children in our learning environments. As pressure to perform mounts in classrooms across America and in many other nations, we see students exhibiting signs of significant stress and emotional instability. Pairing this with the developmental stages the children's brains are going through, and it is a recipe for disaster. What makes this scenario worse is when the children are reinforced through aggressive or psychologically abusive tactics to force performance.

Researchers in Zurich have recently identified how the brain changes in direct correlation to stress. The neurotransmitter noradrenaline is released during times of great stress. When this occurs, it rewires patterns between different regions of the brain (Zerbi et al., 2019). It was also noted that amygdala activity and surrounding networks that process sensory stimuli were increased (Zerbi et al., 2019). The purpose of this reaction is to aid the person in making life-or-death decisions based upon environmental cues (Zerbi et al., 2019). In turn, this efficiently establishes functional networks between various areas of the brain (Zerbi et al., 2019). The areas affected process sensory stimuli in the visual and auditory center of the brain (Zerbi et al., 2019). The amygdala network is associated with states of anxiety. Pairing this with the development of the prefrontal cortex, which as mentioned previously, controls impulsivity and we find the brain operating in a heightened state of stress which will condition the development of the brain itself.

A study done on children who were institutionalized in Romania found that children who were placed in foster care showed better recovery from the adversity, but found that boys overall did not adjust as well as the girls (Zeanah et al., 2009). They found that no manner of intervention changed the long-term psychological trajectory for the boys who spent any time in their formative years institutionalized (Zeanah et al., 2009). Instead, they found increased instances of mental illness into adulthood as a result of this experience where they were not provided adequate nurturing early in life (Zeanah et al., 2009). Although most children in America do not live in orphanages, there are many children who spend far more time in daycare centers than they do in their homes with family members. With the number of children being cared for in any daycare setting, children who are under the age of 5 are not likely to receive the level of intimate nurturing that is essential to healthy psychological brain development.

I have observed daycare scenarios where some children were put into a playpen and then placed in the bathroom so that they did not disturb the other children during nap time. Others would isolate a child in another room to punish them for behavior. Childcare providers spend more time entertaining and feeding the children than they do holding them, making them feel heard, and validating their emotions. Many childcare providers talk to the children in a manner that looks like feigned attention to the child, but they aren't really listening to the child's feelings or points. They may nod their head, say some things that sound like they are listening, but they do not really hear the child. This eventually leads to a child having a tantrum or other unruly behavior to demand to be heard. Then the child is punished for this display of inappropriate behavior. Who is to blame in this scenario?

Researchers Tottenham and colleagues (2009) found that the longer a child is institutionalized, the larger their amygdala volume, which increases emotional regulation difficulties. It has also been identified that a lack of a stable caregiver has been proven to be a potent stressor to developing infants (Johnson, 2002). Although most research has only just begun to focus on the psychological impact of children adopted from orphanages, there remains to be adequate research (or any) done on the impact of childcare centers on the developing brains of infants and toddlers. With the constant changing of staff, it was found that the children in one orphanage found them to have inconsistent nurturing from any one caregiver (Smyke et al., 2007). It was even found that children as young as four months old who experienced such scenarios displayed emotional disruptions which reflected a more heightened emotional reactivity and an increased prevalence of anxiety disorders when compared to those who were cared for by a consistent caregiver during these early formative years (Ames, 1997; Ellis, Fisher, & Zaharie, 2004; Hodges & Tizzard, 1989). Paired with this increased emotional dysregulation, anxiety, and increased amygdala size due to early childhood stress, it is found that it matures the brain faster, but only during this period of development. Maturity in this sense results in inflexibility.

> The brain is the key organ of stress processes. It determines what individuals will experience as stressful, it orchestrates how individuals will cope with stressful experiences, and it changes both functionally and structurally as a result of stressful experiences. Within the brain, a distributed, dynamic, and plastic neural circuitry coordinates, monitors, and calibrates behavioral and physiological stress response systems to meet the demands imposed by particular stressors. These allodynamic processes can be adaptive in the short term (allostasis) and maladaptive in the long term (allostatic load). Critically, these processes involve bidirectional signaling between the brain and body. Consequently, allostasis and allostatic load can jointly affect vulnerability to brain-dependent and stress-related mental and physical health conditions. (McEwan & Gianaros, 2011, Abstract)

Evolutionary response to stress is to prepare the person or animal experiencing the stress to develop more rapidly to survive (Tyborowska et al., 2018).

More personal early-life stressful events were associated with larger developmental reductions in GMV over anterior prefrontal cortex, amygdala and other subcortical regions; whereas ongoing stress from the adolescents' social environment was related to smaller reductions over the orbitofrontal and anterior cingulate cortex. These findings suggest that early-life stress accelerates pubertal development, whereas an adverse adolescent social environment disturbs brain maturation with potential mental health implications: delayed anterior cingulate maturation was associated with more antisocial traits – a juvenile precursor of psychopathy. (Tyborowska et al., 2018, Abstract)

What Tyborowska and colleagues (2018) have identified is that the stress experienced in childhood (0-5) speeds up the cerebral development, yet stress in adolescence (14-17) has the opposite effect. Due to the inflexibility that was developed due to early childhood stress, the adolescent brain is less capable of adjusting to stressors as it cannot adjust for current experiences. The long-term results are increased probability of developing antisocial personality disorders that can range up to full psychopathology. Bloomfield and colleagues (2019) also found that a lifetime of adversity also impairs essential dopamine production to aid one in coping with stressful situations.

Cortisol is another factor that is involved during stressful situations. It is released during moments of stress that result in the fight or flight response. Although, the full responses are more than these two. We will see fight, flight, freeze, and fawn responses in those who are experiencing stressful situations that put them into survival mode. Fight results in obvious aggressive self-defense behavior. Flight means running from a stressful situation. Freeze is observed as someone who cannot decide or do anything when in a stressful situation. Fawn is the person who will please the abuser to survive the situation by being amenable. Cortisol is the key ingredient to all these responses. Those who have experienced childhood trauma have demonstrated DNA level gene expression that had low levels of glucocorticoid receptors, meaning that cortisol is unable to bind to these receptors, thus providing decreased capacity to be resilient to stress (Hyman, 2009). This level of change is then passed on epigenetically to future generations as will be discussed in a later chapter.

So why is the prefrontal cortex, amygdala, and cortisol so important? Other than the previously mentioned developmental effects from stress, it is important to understand how these play a role in healthy brain function and pro-social behavior. One factor is moral judgment. Moral judgment is how one evaluates what is right and wrong based upon social norms (Jonathan, 2003; Prehn et al., 2007). The issue lies in whether the individual makes these moral judgments based upon personal experience or through cognitive processing (Dashtestani et al., 2018). Many studies have demonstrated how some participants make their moral judgments not only on rational thoughts, but also through emotions (Glen, Raine, & Schug, 2009; Greene et al. 2004, 2001; Han, Chen, Jeong, & Glover, 2016; Han, Glover, & Jeong, 2014; Koenigs et al., 2007; Prehn et al., 2007). If one's mind has been developed through stress, it is going to be prone to make emotional decisions before it makes rational ones. The influence of these well-developed patterns will play a pivotal role in decision making.

Researchers have found that children who demonstrate callous behaviors, have different brain structures than those who do not demonstrate these behaviors (Koen et al., 2018). Callous traits are key risk factors for antisocial behavior, which include a lack of empathy, remorselessness, and shallow affect (Hare & Neumann, 2008).

Callous traits in childhood are identified through a broader set of traits relating to unemotional or psychopathic traits as analyzed through a subgroup of children with conduct problems identified by the DSM-5 as low prosocial emotions (American Psychiatric Association, 2013). These traits distinguish themselves through severe and chronic antisocial behavior presentation (Viding & McCrory, 2018). Identification of these traits has proven to be spanned beyond childhood, predicting potential for adult psychopathy, personality disorders, substance abuse, and criminal behavior (Blair, White, Meffert, & Hwang, 2014).

When considering the caretaking experience children have with childcare providers and within their homes, it is important to note these effects on the child's brain development and how that impacts them in the classroom. Many teachers and administrators have resorted to yelling at students to get their attention or to address them for infractions. These responses from the adults are irrespective of the child's brain development or trauma experience. These responses are based upon the programmed responses the adult developed in their own childhood. It is important to note the responsibility any adult has when providing care or education to any child. The effects are lifelong. Researchers from the University of Geneva (UNIGE), Switzerland discovered that people notice what is said to them faster if it is yelled at them than when it is spoken in a normal tone (Burra et al., 2019). The brain identifies the sound as a threat and sends the mind into fight or flight response, thus triggering a trauma response and setting for the previously mentioned brain structure changes (Burra et al., 2019). This is to enable our mind to adapt to a survival threat quickly. If the adults want to be considered a threat to a child's survival, then we are sending the wrong message to children about what adults should represent to them in this world. One would hope that the adults would want the children to feel safe with them and know that they can rely upon the adults to protect and provide for them, not be a source of threat for their very survival. Young minds only know what they are exposed to.

~ 7 ~

NORMALIZED TRAUMA

"It is not the trauma itself that is the source of illness but the uncon-
scious, repressed, hopeless despair over not being allowed to give expres-
sion to what one has suffered and the fact that one is not allowed to show
and is unable to experience feelings of rage, anger, humiliation, despair,
helplessness, and sadness." - Alice Miller

Introduction

When we consider childhood trauma, we often think of physical violence or sexual abuse. Trauma is so normalized in our society, that
we don't often consider the impact of many other factors that cause
long-term trauma such as car accidents, divorce, verbal abuse, or
spanking. Many may think that verbal abuse and spanking aren't
abuse. They consider it discipline. As discussed in the previous chapter, the brain is designed to respond to threat, so physical violence
(such as spanking) or verbal abuse (such as being yelled at) are triggers to rewire the brain to adapt to these experiences as fight or
flight triggers. This eventually creates responses such as hypervigilance, anxiety, and inability to concentrate. Pair this with institutional mandatory active shooter drills, earthquake drills, and the

like. Add childhood bullies, aggressive teachers, or parents who mock their children. The media, especially social media, supports even more traumatic exposure. It's everywhere and it is normalized.

Researchers have found that childhood trauma is far more common than previously understood. William E. Copeland, Ph.D. and colleagues with the Vermont Center for Children, Youth and Families at the University of Vermont were part of The Great Smoky Mountain Study, a study of 1,420 children in 11 rural North Carolina counties. Through 11,000 interviews spanning from 1993 until 2015, demonstrated that 60 percent of study participants were exposed to at least one trauma by the time they were 16 years of age and more than 30 percent of participants had experienced more than one traumatic event (Copeland et al,, 2018).

> Among the 1420 study participants, 630 (49.0%) were female and 983 (89.4%) were white. By age 16 years, 30.9% of children (n = 451) were exposed to 1 traumatic event, 22.5% (n = 289) were exposed to 2 such events, and 14.8% (n = 267) were exposed to 3 or more. Cumulative childhood trauma exposure to age 16 years was associated with higher rates of adult psychiatric disorders (odds ratio for any disorder, 1.2; 95% CI, 1.0-1.4) and poorer functional outcomes, including key outcomes that indicate a significantly disrupted transition to adulthood (eg, failure to hold a job and social isolation). Childhood trauma exposure continued to be associated with higher rates of adult psychiatric and functional outcomes after adjusting for a broad range of childhood risk factors, including psychiatric functioning and family adversities and hardships (adjusted odds ratio for any disorder, 1.3; 95% CI, 1.0-1.5). (Copeland et al., 2018, p. 1)

Prevalence of trauma for other groups will be further discussed in the chapter on epigenetics. However, a study by Tanya N. Alim and colleagues (2006) found:

> Trauma exposure is high in African Americans who live in stressful urban environments. Posttraumatic stress disorder (PTSD) and depression are common outcomes of trauma exposure and are understudied in African Americans....Our study evaluated trauma exposure, PTSD and major depression in African Americans attending primary care offices. METHOD: Six-hundred-seventeen patients (96% African Americans) were surveyed for trauma exposure in the waiting rooms of four primary care offices. Those patients reporting significant traumatic events were invited to a research interview. Of the 403 patients with trauma exposure, 279 participated. RESULTS: Of the 617 participants, 65% reported > or = 1 clearly traumatic event. The most common exposures were transportation accidents (42%), sudden unexpected death of a loved one (39%), physical assault (30%), assault with a weapon (29%) and sexual assault (25%). Lifetime prevalence of PTSD and a major depressive episode (MDE) among those with trauma exposure (n=279) was 51% and 35%, respectively. The percent of lifetime PTSD cases (n=142) with comorbid MDE was 46%. Lifetime PTSD and MDE in the trauma-exposed population were approximately twice as common in females than males, whereas current PTSD rates were similar. CONCLUSIONS: Our rate of PTSD (approximately 33% of those screened) exceeds estimates for the general population. Rates of

MDE comorbid with PTSD were comparable to other studies. (p. 1630)

Extensive research into other populations would show similar findings. America is a melting pot population that is frequently segregated by race for statistics. Often, the White population is considered more protected than the rest. African Americans also have a history of deeper abuses experienced in previous generations, as do Native Americans. African Americans, Latinos and Native Americans increased effects from trauma are often due to systemic racism, discrimination, and micro-aggressions. The chapter on Epigenetics will discuss these populations in more depth.

Common Traumas

DOMESTIC VIOLENCE

The most common trauma would be domestic violence. The prevalence of it in America is quite high. Family and domestic health violence estimates place 10 million people affected annually, and it is also noted to be under-reported (Huecker & Smock, 2019). Abuse ranges from physical, sexual, emotional, economic, and psychological and is done to persons of any age (Huecker & Smock, 2019). This means that exposure to it is nearly impossible to avoid. Children who may not experience it at home, may experience it in a friend's home, or through classroom experiences. Teachers who are experiencing it at home will also likely find it runs into their workplace experience and they may not treat children or coworkers the way they would if they were not experiencing domestic violence at home. This can vary from demonstrating bully behavior themselves all the way to having no boundaries and allowing adults and children to bully them as it is a conditioned response to threat. Children and adults are all prone to the effects of domestic violence regardless of their proximity to the source of the violence.

> Domestic violence affects the victim, families, co-workers, and community. It causes diminished psychological and physical health, decreases the quality of life, and results in decreased productivity. The national economic cost of domestic and family violence is estimated to be over 12 billion dollars per year." (Huecker & Smock, 2019, p. 1)

Domestic violence is found across all racial, ethnic, and socioeconomic groups. This means that it is a nationwide issue irrespective of community and economic capacity. Witnessing abuse also causes the same degree of mental health harm as experiencing the abuse directly (Tsavoussis et al., 2014). Another factor that is found to be commonly tied to premature aging and poor outcomes for children when they reach adulthood, are those who were raised in environments where one or both parents are considered "cold."

PARENTS, CAREGIVERS, AND TEACHERS
Just as early life stress can impact brain development, lack of essential affection can also play a role in the psychological development of a child as much as it also offers increased outcomes that result in physical disease, premature aging, and early death (Knutsen et al., 2019). The way in which parents, caregivers, or teachers communicate with children can also trigger trauma (La Buissonnière-Ariza et al., 2019). Harsh parenting, as described by researchers La Buissonnière-Ariza and colleagues (2019) includes yelling, spanking, shaking them, or expressing anger frequently. They also found that the effects could be seen through the children's teenage years and beyond.

Harsh parenting affects the way in which teenage brains process fear, thus affecting behavior (La Buissonnière-Ariza et al., 2019). This processing of fear is later translated to adult anxiousness, which has been shown to be passed down from parent to child, and likely any adult caretaker or teacher to child as a child is very impressionable and their mind is in a constant state of learning to adapt to the environment for survival (Chang & Debiec, 2016).

It would make sense that a child would learn survival instincts from those who are responsible for their caretaking. Their immediate surroundings and exposure correlate with what their brain needs to adapt to in order to survive. Pairing this with DNA programmed epigenetic trauma inheritance, and the child will adapt more readily to what their brain will deem as potential threats based upon their DNA, environment, and the behavior of those around them.

PEERS
This leads to the next most influential aspect on a child's psychological development through exposure. Peer involvement has been known to be influential primarily on teenage risk taking. This is the age where most parents are more concerned about the influence of peers on their children's decisions. At this juncture, parents will be more mistrustful, put more pressure on their child to resist the peer pressure they may encounter, and amplified attempts to control the child occur. Peer influence alone cannot be considered without the correlation of the adult caretaker's role in this influence.

Another aspect that has become increasingly more visible due to social media and larger online footprints by children and adults alike is victimization. The way in which a child is victimized by those of their own age group, peer group, and adults has grown exponentially due to the advent of the Internet. It is not as though these behaviors did not exist before; however, they are far more prolific and less hidden as they had been previously. What would have been the school bully and their group of friends, is now random strangers on the Internet banding together to attack random people due to any number of reasons why they choose to target an individual. No individual online is shielded from this activity today.

It would be apparent that this type of behavior would also program the developing brain to be more vigilant due to the obvious threatening nature of the behavior the recipient is exposed to. Erin Burke Quinlan and colleagues found that "the experience of chronic peer victimization during adolescence might induce psychopathology-relevant deviations from normative brain development. Early peer victimization interventions could prevent such pathological changes" (2018). Al Race, the Deputy Director of the Center on the Developing Child at Harvard has stated that chronic stress does impact brain development, immune system response, cardiovascular functionality, and metabolic regulation (2020). It is also very likely that students who experience stress at home are more likely to also experience stress at school. However, it is not definitive and there will be exceptions to this. The trouble is that the prevalence of peer victimization leaves no child untouched. Those who experience trauma outside of school will be even more likely to experience dramatic increases in physical and psychological stress responses that will decrease their overall psychological development, physical development, and social development. All of which will impact learning.

One of the most critical aspects in identifying which children are experiencing this degree of trauma is their inability to form meaningful relationships. They are wary of adults, so they do not trust the adults in their world to provide a safe environment that will protect and nurture them. If these adults do not protect them from outside abuse, they are also deemed untrustworthy and as such, are frequently rebelled against.

> We tend to think of trauma as the result of a frightening and upsetting event. But many children experience trauma through ongoing exposure, throughout their early development, to abuse, neglect, homelessness, domestic violence or violence in their communities. And it's clear that chronic trauma can cause serious problems with learning and behavior. (Miller, 2020, para. 1)

These children may find themselves targets of additional abuse from peers due to their inability to form relationships. Some may become bullies and their understanding of relationships is through domination and control. This would have been learned from the way that relationships are formed in their homes, in their community, and even in their classrooms. Many ways they may exhibit these behaviors include poor self-regulation, negative thinking, executive function issues, hypervigilance, and difficulty forming bonds (Miller, 2020).

Big Picture

What we see in our schools is a significant over-diagnosis of Attention Deficit Hyperactivity Disorder or other such labels such as Oppositional Defiance Disorder. The solution is to medicate the child and reinforce behavior through punishment and reward systems, all of which feed directly into future street drug abuse and further reinforcement that their feelings are invalid, thus perpetuating the brain's instinct to self-protect. The fact that these drugs have been used on children long before we even understood the way in which their brains develop in response to trauma is highly unethical and should very much be called into question.

Recent efforts to curb trauma have been the use of meditation and other self-soothing strategies. In fact, every single solution ever suggested is a band-aid rather than a cure to the trauma that we continue to perpetuate for children across America. There have been some studies that have identified that there are some children who appear to be more resilient to maltreatment than others, which is explained by the way their brain networks altered development (Ohashi et al., 2018). What these studies do not include are the other factors in these children's lives that may have compensated for the exposure to trauma.

There have been numerous studies that have pointed to workaholic tendencies appearing on some who respond to stress by working more and dissociating through focus (Reyson et al., 2014). This can also be found through students who dive deeply into literature or the arts. The way in which many school districts across the nation are removing the arts and physical education from their programs in favor of longer class periods focusing on math and other "staple" subjects only reinforces the increased result of more children finding themselves medicated in order to be functional in the classroom.

One way or another, their brain will dissociate. For some, it will be forced medication rather than a choice they would have made for themselves that would very likely be more beneficial and would expand their knowledge and capacity to understand the world around them through artistic expression and exploration. In fact, it is quite easy to find a multitude of research studies that date back for the last 30 years supporting the way in which studying the arts, especially music, actually builds more neurotransmitters in the brain between regions of the brain (Gangrade, 2012).

What is to be done with the children who are facing systemic abuse? They can't escape it no matter where they go. They could be living in a society that is abusive toward them for their appearance, for their lineage, or for the language barrier. Their families may be refugees fleeing war in their homelands and they not only faced trauma from where they came, but also trauma along the journey, only to find themselves further traumatized by the society that was their hope for salvation. Boston Children's Hospital has done an in-depth study on what happens to their brain development and their outcomes in adolescence as a result of their experiences (2018). No manner of education in this realm will change the systemic attitudes of the society they find themselves in seeking refuge. They have been marked as easy prey, and easy prey they will be.

This is further evidence of what family separation can do to a developing mind, yet we find countless examples of family separation in America every single day. Whether this be by divorce, escaping from abuse, or from having the system remove children for what may or may not be actual abuse. It further traumatizes the child beyond the trauma they have already experienced more often than not (D'Onofrio & Emery, 2019).

Long-Term Implications

It would be short-sighted to not consider the long-term implications of childhood trauma and the way it is reinforced through normalized trauma. The long-term trajectory shows increased mental illness and physical diseases into adulthood for many who have experienced childhood trauma (Mock & Arai, 2011). A long-term survey collected data from over 600,000 Americans between 2009-2017 to learn how common mental illness has become. During this time depression in people between 20-21 years of age increased from 7 percent to 15 percent. Those between the ages at 16 and 17 had an increase of depression of 69 percent (Twenge et al., 2019). Those between 18 to 25 years old saw a surge in psychological distress which was found among 71 percent of those surveyed (Twenge et al., 2019). Suicide attempts for those between 22 and 23 doubled and more than 55 percent had suicidal thoughts (Twenge et al., 2019). It was also found that the prevalence of increases was found among girls and young women (Twenge et al., 2019).

Another study in North Carolina with 1,402 participants whom they followed from 9 years of age until 30 stated that,

> Childhood trauma exposure is a common experience that affects boys and girls and different racial/ethnic groups at similar rates. Such exposures are associated with an array of childhood psychiatric problems and other familial hardships and adversities. Our study suggested that childhood trauma casts a long and wide-ranging shadow, showing associations with elevated risk for adult psychiatric status, important domains of functioning (health, risky and/or criminal behavior, financial/educational functioning, and social functioning). This increased risk persisted when accounting for (1) childhood psychiatric problems, (2) other family and individual hardships and adversities, and (3) adult exposure to traumatic events. (Copeland et al., 2018, p. 7)

Copeland and colleagues (2018) also found that cumulative trauma was directly correlated with all manner of diagnosed childhood behavioral disorders and childhood difficulties and hardships (Copeland et al., 2018). The long-term implications are quite clear and deeply studied. There is no lack of evidence to justify a substantial reconsideration of what we are subjecting children to in our classrooms and homes.

As mentioned in the previous chapter, amygdala volume is truncated in adolescent development due to the exposure to trauma or situations that the brain perceives as a threat. It has been found that this also contributes to depressive symptom severity in young adults (Daftary et al., 2018). This study took a sample size of 1,747 adults in Dallas and found that the issue was primarily located in the right portion of the amygdala in participants ranging from 18 - up through adults over 60 years of age (Daftary et al., 2018). What this suggests is that brain development limitations are permanent and as Copeland and colleagues found, will create continuous traumatic experiences throughout adulthood. The long-term effects not only impact the individual, but their current and future relationships.

Trauma is incredibly normalized in American society. It includes abuse and neglect, incarceration, bullying, parental abandonment, chronic unemployment, poverty, death of a loved one, car accidents, domestic violence, substance abuse, and community violence. The national average for adverse childhood experiences (ACE) includes 30 percent of the population with multiple ACE experiences and goes as high as 47 percent in certain segments of the country. Schools holding lockdown drills also contribute to the traumatization of children. The current response to society is to treat it as a dangerous threat. This has escalated over the last century. What used to be closet abuse is now rampant visible abuse on a daily basis. Mere exposure to the daily news is traumatizing at this juncture.

We are also finding increasing examples of narcissistic abuse in leadership roles. Many of these angry people also overestimate their intelligence, which hinders the development of organizations and the potential capacity they may have if their leadership did not exhibit these traits (Zajenkowski & Gignac, 2018). Long-term family stability also relies upon fully developed prefrontal brain activity in order to ensure healthy relationships, which ultimately prevent more trauma from being experienced within the family unit (Ueda et al., 2018). Children who also grow up with targeted and socially supported abuse, such as racism, sexism, etc. also find themselves with increased levels of ACEs scores and predisposition to mental illness. The next chapter will discuss in more depth the role that epigenetic trauma inheritance also plays for those who experienced genocide and other atrocities and how that is visible in today's classrooms.

~ 8 ~

EPIGENETIC TRAUMA
INHERITANCE

Implications in Education

The field of epigenetics, discovering that what our ancestors did and the way that they did it, has implications for students in the classroom. What our ancestors experienced, for example, in terms of famines or other life-threatening scenarios, is passed on to their descendants through their genes. This discovery lends itself to investigate the possibility of epigenetics influencing why some learners could possibly be having trouble in the classroom: it's not the way their ancestors learned. In fact, from many points of view, it would be easy to see the current educational system as oppressive. I define oppressive education as the debilitation of the students' ability to acquire the skills necessary for them to develop their highest self-expression and become a contributing member of society.

Students with relatively more recent tribal ancestry appear to have more difficulties in typical western education (U.S. Department of Education, National Center for Education Statistics, 2010). Certainly, the literature points to a variety of reasons, such as poverty, the lack of parental involvement, etc. (Child Trends Bank, 2010), but it is possible that epigenetic influence is also a significant and over-looked factor.

Epigenetic inheritance is the term defined by Lawrence V. Harper, professor of human development at University of California, Davis, as "the transmission to offspring of parental phenotypic responses to environmental challenges—even when the young do not experience the challenges themselves. Genetic inheritance is not altered, gene expression is" (Harper, 2005, p. 340). Epigenetics, therefore, operates like a light switch. Since all cells in the human body contain identical genetic potential, the differentiating factor is which segments of the genetic code are expressed in each tissue. Certain genes within each cell are turned on or off which can then be passed to further generations without changes in the DNA sequence. Harper also suggests that the light switch in DNA expression may be triggered by environmental stimuli which will affect the genetic expression physically or for behaviors in this lifetime and those of future generations (Harper, 2005). Evolution, therefore, plays a large role in the understanding of epigenetics. In theory, a phenotypic alteration in gene expression, which is an adaptation to environmental demands, would increase the chances of survival. This survival expression would naturally be passed down to future generations to ensure the continuation of the species.

The recent discovery of epigenetics has scientists reeling at the possible implications. Epigenetics suggests that traumatic events that have occurred to our ancestors are currently impacting our lives today (Alder, Fink, Bitzer, Hosli, & Holzgreve, 2007; Bird, 2007; Campbell, Marriott, Nahmias, & MacQueen, 2004; Cerqueira, Pego, Taipa, Bessa, Almeida, & Sousa, 2005; Cole, Hawkley, Arevalo, Sung, Rose, & Cacioppo, 2007; Dalton, Nacewicz, Alexander, & Davidson, 2007; Dalton, Nacewicz, Johnstone, Schaefer, Gernsbacher, Goldsmith, Davidson, 2005; DiPietro, 2009; Fales, Barch, Rundle, Mintun, Snyder,

Cohen, Sheline, 2008; Ganzel, Kim, Glover, & Temple, 2008; Ganzel, Morris, Wethington, 2010; Groome, Swiber, Bentz, Holland, & Atterbury, 1995; Harper, 2005; Jablonka & Lamb, 1995; Jablonka & Raz, 2009; Kaati, Bygren, & Edvinsson, 2002; Kessler, R., Sonnega, Bromet, Hughes, & Nelson, 1995; Masterpasqua, 2009; McGowan, Sasaki, D'Alessio, Dymov, Labonte, Szyf, J., et al., 2009; Meaney, 2001; Meaney, 2004; Meaney, Szyf, & Seckl, 2007; Mennes, Van den Bergh, Lagae, & Stiers, 2009; Mill & Petronis, 2008; Moffitt, Caspi & Rutter, 2006; Oberlander, Weinberg, Papsdorf, Grunau, Misri, & Devlin, 2008; Pray, 2006; Richards, 2006; Susser, Hoek, & Brown, 1998; Szyf, McGowan, & Meaney, 2008; Van den Bergh, 2010; Weaver, Cervoni, Champagne, D'Alessio, Sharma, Seckl, Meaney, 2004; Yehuda, Bierer, Schmeidler, Aferiat, Breslau, & Dolan, 2000;). The research is currently focusing on diseases, and implications in psychological development is now being considered. I would like to consider the implications of this in education

Students who statistically succeed utilizing standardized examinations have historically been of Asian or Caucasian descent (National Assessment of Educational Progress data, 2007). Those who have statistically fared less successfully are often African and Native American students (among other recent historically tribal cultures). A recent study found that after careful analysis of 6,000 twins in the United Kingdom, educational achievement was "highly heritable across school years and across subjects studied [and] achievement is highly stable.....genetic factors accounted for most of this stability (70%) even after controlling for intelligence (60%)" (Rimfeld et al., 2018). I would like to offer a theory which may influence our current approach to school reform. I begin with understanding the suggestion of epigenetics playing a role in their learning styles.

Epigenetics suggest that traumatic events turn the genetic switch so that future generations are able to handle similar circumstances more effectively than their ancestors. Traumatic events can include anything from famine to war. Isolating two specific groups, the African and Native American peoples have similar traumatic experiences in the United States. One group was forced to leave their homeland and forced into slavery, the other was encroached upon and many of their people were annihilated. Both groups were forced to attend boarding schools in America. Both were expected to forget their roots and adapt to the new European settler's way of life. The children were removed from their homes and tribes and were forced into boarding schools that stripped them of their culture, their language, and their way of life. I believe that this common traumatic experience may epigenetically affect their learning today.

It could be suggested that these two groups have an epigenetically instinctual resistance to the cultures who subjected their ancestors to such trauma. Another factor to consider is that their indigenous pre-colonized way of life is still epigenetically ingrained in who they are. Their pre-colonized existence was often not ecologically or environmentally destructive (Lewis, 1995). The industrialized compulsory education machine that took over their lives in the mid-1800's is very contradictory to their deeply rooted philosophies on coexistence with nature. The goal of the original compulsory schools was to create factory workers for the industrial revolution. This industrial revolution contributed greatly to many incredible inventions. It also contributed greatly to massive destruction and pollution of our earth. I believe the African and Native American peoples' deeply ingrained epigenetic instinct, from thousands of years of tribal life that respected the earth, could play a role in their instinctive resistance to our factory model education system. The way that they educated their young pre-colonization is also another epigenetic factor to consider.

Epigenetics: Adaptation to Western Educational Methods

The study of epigenetics is not new, it was first suggested a millennia ago. The earliest extant discussion was by ancient Greek philosophers. The idea gained popularity again with Alfred Russell Wallace when he and Darwin discussed the concept of evolution by natural selection in 1859. Before Darwin, Lamarck addressed the idea in earnest only to be challenged by Weismann in 1880. Prior to the 1990's, the scientific community consistently rejected the theory as its ability to analyze the genome and gene expression did not arrive until later (Wallace, 1893; Joffe 1969; Jablonka & Raz, 2009; Rakyan & Beck, 2006). In terms of a definition, epigenetics, as defined by Bird, is "the structural adaptation of chromosomal regions so as to register, signal, or perpetuate altered activity states" (Bird, 2007, p. 398). This includes environmental impacts on genetic expression. It is important to understand that the DNA structure itself is not altered, it is the expression of the gene that changes and sometimes to varying degrees (Harper, 2005; Pray, 2006). In some cases, the expression is even silenced, also known as methylation (Harper, 2005; Pray, 2006; Ganzel, Morris, & Wethington, 2010).

As stated previously, epigenetics operates like a light switch. Since all cells in the human body contain identical genetic potential, the differentiating factor is which segments of the genetic code are expressed in each tissue. Certain genes within each cell are turned on or off which can then be passed to further generations without changes in the DNA sequence. Harper also suggests, as mentioned previously, that the light switch in DNA expression may be triggered by environmental stimuli which will affect the genetic expression physically or for behaviors in this lifetime and those of future generations (Harper, 2005).

Evolution, therefore, plays a large role in the understanding of epigenetics. In theory, a phenotypic alteration in gene expression, which is an adaptation to environmental demands, would increase the chances of survival. This survival expression would naturally be passed down to future generations to ensure the continuation of the species. Jablonca and Lamb (1995) have reviewed a large body of evidence showing that, from protozoa to mammals, selection has indeed favored the intergenerational transmission of modifications in gene expression. The genome itself is not altered; the degree of expression of inherited potentials for tracking an environment is influenced by events impinging on the parent. The evidence indicates that when certain aspects of an individual's inherited range of reaction are expressed in response to events in the environment, the resulting epigenetic states may be transmitted, not just to daughter cells in that individual, but across generations (see also Rossiter, 1996) (Harper, 2005).

Until the discovery of epigenetics, research on evolutionary genetics focused on random DNA mutations. In the light of epigenetics, however, this theory no longer has any basis for merit. The concept of epigenetics influencing human evolution provides a clearer understanding of observed changes in DNA expression. Lamarck suggested that the human body would adapt to the conditions it was living in. This trait could then be passed down intergenerationally, providing a supporting idea for the evolutionary theory of Darwin. The theory goes that if an organ or appendage is used, that strengthening or weakening of the organ or appendage would be passed down to future generations. As an example, from our own personal experience, modern humans have body parts (appendix, wisdom teeth, etc.) that are no longer serving a function, yet we still have them in our bodies.

There is now substantial research demonstrating that alterations in the epigenetic patterns surrounding DNA plays an essential role in the normal development of human beings, as well as in the etiology of a number of diseases. These patterns are dynamic within the lifespan of the individual, may be influenced by experience, and, in some instances, may be transferred to subsequent generations. While epigenetic inheritance across more than one generation has been observed in mice exposed to prenatal chemical and nutritional changes, the evidence for transgenerational effects in humans, although suggestive, has yet to be corroborated by controlled studies. Nevertheless, these results suggest that the consequences of an individual's lifestyle may extend beyond their own mortality to include their descendants (Masterpasqua, F., 2009). In our current psychological view, behavioral development of individuals is perceived as the direct result of genetics, culture, and parental practices (nature and nurture). We now have epigenetic inheritance as an additional contributor.

While the Human Genome Project provided a complete map of the DNA sequence, it was not designed to take into account gene expression. One of these researchers, Masterpasqua, expressed "epigenetics is defined as mechanisms of gene expression that can be maintained across cell divisions, and thus the life of the organism, without changing the DNA sequence" (Masterpasqua, 2009, p. 194). This research has provided us with the understanding of how epigenetics influences the physical and psychological development of multiple generations of descendants. The implications of this, how environmental and psychosocial factors are changing the epigenome, provide us with suggestions of monumental significance (Masterpasqua, 2009). These implications not only create new perspectives on the treatment of physical and behavioral disorders, but suggest new areas of exploration as we realize that the results of our current choices as well as our responses to environmental impacts that are carried into the future by our very genes, outliving one body and carrying on in the next.

Epigenetics: Survival

The research on epigenetic inheritance is beginning to demonstrate that changes in gene expression are especially evident during repetitively traumatic environmental experiences, like cycles of famine. These occurrences do not necessarily have to happen in one singular lifetime, but if they occur repeatedly in future generations, are unpredictable, and uncontrollable by the affected persons, then they tend to be highly likely to be epigenetically passed down. Situations involving famine or forcible subjugation are prominent areas where changes in gene expression are created. Such circumstances can create intergenerational epigenetically inherited changes in phenotypic response. The traumatic circumstances do not have to be present in those future generations for this genetic expression to continue to occur. The number of generations affected can be numerous before the phenotypic gene expression reverts to its original state prior to the traumatic experience (Jablonca & Lamb, 1995; e.g., Zamenhof, vanMarthens & Grael, 1971; e.g., Lumey & Stein, 1997; Szyf et al., 2008).

Key factors that contribute to generational changes in phenotypic response include the severity of the environmental threat, how unpredictable it is and the variability of the threat. The individual needs to be able to develop a reliable response to a detectable cue which reduces the opportunity for injury and therefore increases chances for survival. This form of defense becomes an anticipated response prior to the imminent reality of the threat. This ultimately mitigates a more damaging experience than if it were inspired during or after a materialized trauma (Harvell & Tollrain, 1999).

Epigenetics: Pain Memory

Newer scientific studies are focusing on how the emotional state of a pregnant woman could impact the genomic expression of her child. Most of the research focuses on behavioral disorders thought to be generated by the mother's negative emotional states. It is now fair to suggest that the emotional fight or flight experience of the mother can influence genetic expression in the child's developing brain. This does not necessarily have to suggest a behavior disorder, but more importantly an instinctive response to certain circumstances (e.g., DiPietro, 2009; Groome, Swiber, Bentz, Holland, & Atterbury, 1995; Sjöström, Valentin, Thelin, & Marsal, 2002; Van den Bergh, 1990, 1992; Van den Bergh, Mulder, Visser, Poelmann-Weesjes, Bekedam et al., 1989; for reviews, see Alder, Fink, Bitzer, Hosli, & Holzgreve 2007; Mennes, Van den Bergh, Lagae, & Stiers, 2009; Talge, Neal, & Glover, 2007; Van den Bergh, Mulder, Mennes, & Glover, 2005; Van den Bergh, Van Calster, Smits, Van Huffel, & Lagae, 2008; Weinstock, 2008; Meaney, Szyf, & Seckl, 2007).

Just as convincing is the research on the parenting style of a parent who was traumatized as a child. The abuse experienced by the parent also impacts the emotional development of their child, who does not experience the trauma the parent did. Studies have shown that adult children of Holocaust survivors have greater instances of Post-Traumatic Stress Syndrome/Disorder (PTSS/PTSD) than their parents. In fact, these studies have demonstrated that the children of these Holocaust survivors have a higher incidence of PTSD and other mood and anxiety disorders than other demographically similar persons (Yehuda, Bierer, Schmeidler, Aferiat, Breslau, & Dolan, 2000).

As mentioned, one potential mechanism for the increased prevalence of mood and anxiety disorders is altered HPA axis physiology. Children of Holocaust survivors have significantly lower 24-h urinary cortisol secretion when compared with control participants, and offspring of holocaust-surviving parents with PTSD had lower cortisol levels than offspring of Holocaust survivors that did not manifest PTSD (Yehuda et al., 2000). In addition, adult children of Holocaust survivors who manifested PTSD exhibit enhanced cortisol negative feedback inhibition in response to a dexamethasone suppression test (DST; Yehuda, Blair, Labinsky, & Bierer, 2007). Collectively, these data demonstrate that abuse can alter HPA axis activity and risk of psychiatric disorder at least one generation removed from the trauma exposure (Neigh, G.N., Gillespie, C.F., Nemeroff, C.B., 2009). The same was found when studying the transmission of Complex PTSD in the children of Tutsi genocide survivors.

> We need to understand that genocide and massive trauma can leave their mark not only on survivors who were directly exposed, but also on their offspring and probably on other family relatives, as well. We also know from previous studies that the effects of trauma may extend across several generations and linger for decades after the focal trauma took place. (Mollov et.al, 2019, p. 121)

Michael Meaney and his colleagues have done extensive research using animal models of parenting. The parenting itself impacts both the neural development and gene expression of the young with that parental model being passed down through generations of youth by epigenetic inheritance (Meaney, 2001). Another recent study provided potential evidence of a specific type of gene expression in the brains of people who committed suicide. The difference was found systematically to be dependent upon the abuse experienced in the subjects' childhoods (McGowan et al., 2009).

In the physical context, experiences such as famine can affect the physical health of future generations. A study was done in 1997 that focused on the famine which occurred during World War II in the Netherlands. Thanks to detailed records that were collected during this time, researchers were able to trace the long-term and intergenerational transmission of the effects of the trauma of famine experienced perinatally. The traits that were passed down to the grandchildren included "low birth weight, infant mortality, obesity, diabetes, coronary heart disease, cancer, and increased rates of schizophrenia and diagnosis of schizoid personality disorder in the exposed group" (Lumey & Stein, 1997).

Other studies were completed in 2002 and 2006 which focused on harvest and food price records to see if food availability in 1890, 1905 and 1920, in a small Swedish town, had any influence on future mortality rates. What they discovered was that the effects continued through two generations. Sex-specific reactions were also identified. What the paternal grandfathers experienced affected only the grandsons and the same gender specific result was found in the women. These researchers' findings add a new, multi-generational dimension to the interplay between inheritance and environment in health and development; they provide proof of principle that sex-specific, male-line trans-generational effects exist in humans (Pembrey et al., 2006).

While epigenetic research is still ongoing, it is becoming more and more crucial in various universities and medical research facilities. There is sure to be much more discussion in the future regarding the impact that epigenetics plays on our daily living experiences, life expectancies, parenting practices, and how such knowledge can very easily be transferred into areas of focus such as education. Clearly this is a complex area of research that involves much more than mere genetic science. As we have seen, the experience of our parents as well as of the lives before us impacts both our physical and mental health today, while our experiences will impact the lives of generations to come.

Current educational reform focuses on standardized examinations, rote memorization, fact regurgitation and does not promote self-discovery, connection to the earth and all living beings or intrinsic motivation. This focus perpetuates the cycle of consumerism in our world and destroys the cultural understandings and ways of living for indigenous peoples. There is an imbalance occurring that is literally consuming our planet. Adding the concept of epigenetic influence on educational outcomes adds to the concern. The epigenetic phenomenon may be causing two problems:

- Those whose tribal ancestry is still serving in their gene expression will continue to "fail" according to maladaptive systems and suffer accordingly.
- Those who are adapting will likely pass on genes that continue to promote the maladaptations that are causing our world to be out of balance.

For those who are experiencing stronger epigenetic influence counter to Western educational theories, success will remain fleeting. Classroom behavior may represent instinctual resistance to authoritarian structure based upon epigenetic pain memory or due to the inherent knowledge that the disconnect from the earth and their authentic self may very well lead to the destruction of the planet or themselves. True understanding of their culture, their ways of learning and teaching, and respecting their belief systems are necessary for true educational reform to find success. Not only is understanding necessary, action involving their historic learning and knowing methodologies are crucial.

For those who are adapting to the Westernized education system, they will lose their instinctual indigenous knowledge which in turn will perpetuate the imbalance occurring on our planet today. Our world will also lose the knowledge that only they possess. Current educational reform represents a psychological holocaust for these cultures.

~ 9 ~

THE PURPOSE BEHIND
EDUCATION

WHAT PURPOSE DOES STUDYING HOW CHILDREN LEARN SERVE,

IF NOT FOR THE INTENT TO MANIPULATE?

Introduction

There is much that has been said about the purpose of education, especially since the 1970's. The rise in people who are questioning the
education system's purpose and their willingness to participate has
grown substantially in the last 50 years. Homeschooling alone has
grown significantly in the last 20 years. It is no longer something that
is considered a religious focus. It is a resistance to the way in which
the education system treats, educates, and fails to protect children.
It is also the way in which the education system has increased its demands, while consistently failing to improve outcomes, and destroying what was once treasured family time. How did it get to be this
way?

As was discussed in previous chapters, school was never designed
with the family or the individual in mind. Its sole purpose was ini-

tially to serve the Emperor or King and then later used to pre-program children for industrial revolution employer needs. One cannot also ignore the fact that compulsory education was not enacted until 10 years after the abolition of slavery in the United States. Prior to this, there were small schools, but they were not mandatory, and they usually only served those who planned to take on roles of leadership (usually the children of prominent families). Private tutors were also not uncommon prior to this. Learning was always happening. It was not always available to the poor.

The poor frequently had their children working to help support the entire family's survival. Businesses employed children to cut expenses (United States Department of Labor, 2017). Paired with the compulsory education laws, child labor was soon banned. Although it was likely done to protect children, it was ultimately a mere redirection of the children to prepare for future employment while also taking away earnings from the family. To gain support from these families, promises of better lives had to be made. Without this, there would have been riots.

Child Labor

Child labor was not eradicated quickly in the United States. As a result of Puritanism in New England, the belief that children needed education in order to read the Bible was aggressively purported (Trattner, 1970). This took precedence over the horrid conditions and tireless hours that the children were working (Trattner, 1970). Secularists were just as adamant about education to support the idea that an educated citizenship was essential to maintaining democracy (Trattner, 1970). What neither group understood was the way in which education had been utilized to program citizens for governmental purposes for centuries previously. This would become a critical factor in the 20th century. Many governments utilized education to provide propaganda education to perpetuate beliefs that would assist them in their goals (Wooddy, 1935). Many would soon become communist or fascist dictatorship states.

So how did compulsory education in the United States really start? In 1813, the Connecticut legislature passed a law that would require that all child factory workers must be educated in reading, writing, and arithmetic (Trattner, 1970). The parents' rights to raise their children according to their own desires were ignored by this law, which was passed by more states by 1850 (Trattner, 1970). The National Trades' Union called for a factory worker minimum age requirement in 1836, which was followed by further legislation in Massachusetts limiting the number of hours children under age 12 could work (Trattner, 1970). The limit was 10 hours per workday. Connecticut's response was similar, but applied to children under 14 (Trattner, 1970). All New England states had similar laws by 1850 (Felt, 1965). These limited regulations covered children under varying age ranges, depending upon the state. Those ranges went as low as only including children under 9 years of age (Trattner, 1970). None of these laws did anything to stop or prevent child labor.

Public Concern

Child welfare in the 19th century focused exclusively on the issue of vagrant and idle children (Zelizer, 1994). The concern for the child worker wasn't truly focused on until after 1870, due to the large numbers of child laborers represented in the census of 1870 (Trattner, 1970). The use of children in industry became a national platform for the Prohibition Party in 1872, but no widespread support could be found (Trattner, 1970). Child safety became a concern after reports of children being burned alive, suffocated, or died in an attempt to flee a factory fire in 1874 (Trattner, 1970). This only brought focus on safety in factories, not on the number of children working in the factory, despite some of those children being as young as 5 years old (United States Department of Labor, 2017). Child worker numbers continued to increase in the United States. By 1890, 18% of all children between the ages of 10 and 15 were employed (Wood, 2011). Children in northern states found more enrollment of students in secondary school, whereas children in the south remained employed. The north saw a 150% increase in secondary school enrollment between 1890-1900, and the south only had a 21% increase during the same time period (Wood, 2011). Compulsory education laws were being implemented outside of the South post-Civil War (Troen, 1976).

Early Education Reform

The period between 1902 and 1906 saw tremendous increase in publications against child labor and the health concerns for children in the workforce (Trattner, 1970). The push for education, more specifically for the purposes of reading the Bible to lead a moral life, was also reinforced by those attempting to protect children from abusive work environments. Reformers began shifting the public focus from viewing child labor as "beneficent social institution" to "an unrighteous and harmful consequence of industrial capitalism, destructive to the child and community" (Wood, 1968, p.6). Parents, industry, and even children opposed the education reform.

Reform in the South was led by Edgar Gardner Murphy, a clergyman from Arkansas, who founded the National Child Labor Committee (NCLC) in 1904. This was the first true effort from the South to address child labor restrictions and his efforts prompted legislation efforts across many states. His organization supported nationwide efforts to assist individual states with what he drew up as the model child labor bill. This bill declared a minimum working age of 14 years old for manufacturing work and 16 years old for mining labor. Workday hours were limited to 8 per day, no night work allowed, and proof of age was required (Trattner, 1970).

In the North, Mary Harris "Mother Jones" took up the cause alongside the 10,000 children who left their mill work to strike in Kensington, PA in 1903. Her efforts generated public demonstrations and marches that provided public awareness of the physical injuries endured by children working in the mills. She attempted to get the attention of President Theodore Roosevelt, but he determined the cause to be a state issue and that "under the Constitution, Congress had no power to act" (Haines Mofford, 1997). However, Roosevelt did raise the issue of child labor in his State of the Union address to Congress in 1901, and 1904 through 1908. He did not recommend a federal law but emphasized national rules to be passed down to the state level for implementation (Hindman, 2002).

What became a new strategy by the NCLC was to focus on the welfare of children by demonstrating the dangerous work conditions, greed of mill owners, and the irresponsibility of the children's parents. Fathers who were not working due to alcoholism and mothers were painted in a negative light as neglectful and selfish, wanting to wear finery at the toil of their children (Schmidt, 2010). The Wisconsin Child Labor Committee determined that the parents were to blame for all violation of the child labor laws (Wisconsin Child Labor Committee, 1907). Some parents used their children as their financial sustenance, while others competed with children for work (Addams, 1925; Nearing, 1925). The cost of hiring a child was less expensive, usually three times cheaper than the price of hiring an adult (Hindman, 2002). Some parents had doctors write notes stating that the child was unable to attend school due to a handicap, but was then later found working in the coal mine and supervisors never asked for age certificates, especially if they felt sorry for the family (Lovejoy, 1907). Physical abuse by employers was not uncommon (Trattner, 1970). Night work was utilized by business owners who wanted to put fear into the children who did not want to be caught working (Hindman, 2002). Some factories were also surrounded by barbed wire to prevent children from running away (Van Der Vaart, 1907). Most of the children working in the mills were illiterate (Trattner, 1970). Mill workers on the whole were against government regulation of child labor (Trattner, 1970).

A federal child labor bill was introduced to Congress by Republican Senator Albert J. Beveridge of Indiana in 1906. This bill outlawed the transportation of any items produced by child labor between states (Coenen, 2004). This was arguably the most constructive way in which to circumvent the ways that mill and manufacturing owners would violate state laws and also prevent them from hiring underage children who would willingly cross state lines to do work illegal in their own states (Miller, 1907; Beveridge, 1907; & Wood, 1968). This bill was the first to tip the conversation into meaningful and impactful reform. This does not, however, stop the topic of poverty, orphaned children, and those whose parents are too ill to work. Passing laws at the state level was minimal by 1912. Enforcement was often lax and every state violated age-limit laws (Lindenmeyer, 1997). Public concern was minimal, and some manufacturers felt the need to violate the laws in order to economically compete (Watson, 1910).

It was determined that the only way to reinforce compliance with child labor laws was to reinforce the compulsory education laws

(Davies, 1907). At the time, only 80 percent of children 14 years of age were attending school (McCune Lindsay, 1907). The NCLC found that "school authorities are able to do more through their ability to hold children back from work than a whole army of inspectors" (Felt, 1965, p. 86). Concern that children would not attend school if child labor laws were not enforced concurrently with compulsory school attendance was expressed by mill owners (Hindeman, 2002). There was an understanding that children should only work or go to school, anything else was unacceptable. This is important to note as it speaks of the views of children at the time. Encouraging play and exploration of the world was not important. It was about economic productivity alone.

Child labor and compulsory school attendance laws had been enacted in states as early as 1903 (Davies, 1907). However, after turning age 14, only 40% of children went into employment after completing their school requirements. Parents who kept their children at home felt that work was more important than school (Gibbons, 1925). Children also expressed preference of work over school in a 1909 survey of children working in various factories around Chicago (Todd, 1925). They preferred knowing that they were helping the family over spending time sitting in a room learning things they felt were unimportant to them. Propaganda materials that reinforced the increased wage potential for those who attended school were then utilized to encourage the families against schooling to choose schooling for their children (Sallee, 2004). Money is what most people paid attention to. Promise of increased wealth.

The Keating-Owen bill, which emancipated children from labor, was passed and signed into law by President Woodrow Wilson on September 1, 1916 (Trattner, 1970). The law only affected 150,000 out of 1,850,000 employed children nationwide (Trattner, 1970). Those affected worked in quarries, mills, factories, mines, and interstate commerce. Those who worked on the streets, from their homes, or in the fields were left unaffected. The Keating-Owen Act was later struck down by the Supreme Court two years later. A series of acts were to follow, including taxation and an attempted constitutional amendment to outlaw child labor. They were all found unconstitutional. The first child labor law to be left standing was the Fair Labor Standards Act, passed in 1938 (The United States Department of Labor, 2017). However, this law only addressed 850,000 children working in 1938 as some child labor types were not covered by the legislation. Additionally, the national standard of living had improved by that point in time and families could afford to send their children to school (Zelizer, 1994). This was a turning point in the nation, where the expectation that a man would provide for his wife and children took precedence over having his wife and children working. Immigration also impacted the hiring practices of the labor market due to increased immigrants fleeing the wars in Europe arriving with skills that were in demand (Zelizer, 1994; Rosenberg, 2013). This only changed when wartime production needs and labor shortages pressured President Roosevelt to encourage older children to work. Employed children ranged from one to three million in the 1940s (Lindenmeyer, 1997). Child labor protections had to be reversed to accomplish the labor demands at that time. This exception has been very exclusive to the demands of World War II and have not been seen since. That does not mean that children under the "legal" limits have not been employed, they are simply not included in the Bureau of Labor statistical reporting.

School Reform History

Schools in America began as early as the 17th century but were uncommon. By the latter part of the 18th century, through the end of the 19th century, much had changed. The consistent basic focus areas were reading, writing, and arithmetic. Teachers were also required to know Latin. If the teacher had these skills, they were hired. Teachers were predominantly men until shortages became an issue. Many men only looked at teaching as a steppingstone before they began their real careers in law or the church (Pinto, 2019). Small towns would frequently find farmers or even innkeepers at the front of the classroom (Pinto, 2019). Students faced changing teacher realities as the employment and seasons impacted the access to a teacher.

The early 1800's began the first real reform, which is known as the Common School Era. "The grammar schoolteachers have rarely had any education beyond what they have acquired in the very schools where they have to teach. Their attainments, therefore, to say the least, are usually very moderate." -- James Carter, Education Reformer, 1826 (Pinto, 2019). This led to the rise of the education reformer, one of whom was Horace Mann.

Horace wished for a more democratic, universal, and non-sectarian educational experience for students. He joined forces with Henry Barnard, Catharine Beacher, and James Carter to also improve the quality of teachers. This led to the beginning of female educators. By changing society's acceptance of women working outside of the home, more stable teacher experiences could be accomplished and this also led to school districts realizing they could pay the teacher 1/3rd of what they paid a man for the same job. "God seems to have made woman peculiarly suited to guide and develop the infant mind, and it seems...very poor policy to pay a man 20 or 22 dollars a month, for teaching children the ABCs, when a female could do the work more successfully at one third of the price." -- Littleton School Committee, Littleton, Massachusetts, 1849 (Pinto, 2019).

The term Common School was coined for the acknowledgment that anyone, regardless of religion or social class, could attend. These new districts provided schools were the first to be funded through taxes and parent fees. Prior to this, most education came from religious private schools where tuition was required, and many were unable to afford the fees.

Other changes included broader education topics such as social philosophy and common political principals (Pinto, 2019). The goal was to help prevent political instability and upheaval that could destabilize the communities and the nation. Teaching students democratic principles was critical to achieving this aim. Due to the increased numbers of schools, the education of many female teachers took place through formalized teacher training through Normal Schools (Pito, 2019). The appeal included that women were by nature maternal and would nurture high moral character in the students. "The school committee are sentinels stationed at the door of every school house in the State, to see that no teacher crosses its threshold, who is not clothed, from the crown of his head to the sole of his foot, in garments of virtue." --Horace Mann, 1840 (Pinto, 2019). Expectation was that the teachers would provide an exemplary example of upright living.

Classroom management was a concern as the reformers doubted women's ability to maintain order and to discipline students. Many of the female teachers were merely 14 or 15 years old. Older male students would flirt, tease, or disobey them (Pinto, 2019). Additional concern was also focused on the intellectual capacity of females. Many were more educated than previously. As such, requirements were placed upon the teachers to meet certain academic competence and ongoing training attendance (Pinto, 2019). Normal Schools were then developed to ensure the proper training of teachers to address the concerns brought up by the school reformers. Eventually, the training was moved to colleges and universities.

The latter half of the 19th century had better trained teachers, but the curriculum had not become more demanding. Classrooms had up to 60 students in the one-room schoolhouse. The work was challenging for the teachers due to the large groups of non-age-segregated classes. The only major change to the curriculum was the addition of history and a little geography. Morals and virtues were still a predominant fixture in the daily curriculum, which also included the Bible. Women were excited to have the opportunity for independence and to have more access to political and other information that would have been out of their daily experience without teaching. Women could affect change. They were considered outsiders. They developed associations and friendships, which contributed to community transformations. The way that women were viewed changed just as much as the way the women viewed themselves. Liberation and growth for women began.

Additional changes that occurred because of the Common School included the liberation of other groups of people who had previously been cut off from education access. Freed slaves were being prepared to participate in a post-Civil War society. Former slaves were taught literacy, economic independence, and civil rights. The Hampton Institute was founded in 1868 to provide vocational training to Black Americans. The focus was on manual skills rather than academic pursuits. The Indian Department was launched shortly thereafter. The turn of the 20th century brought floods of immigrants who needed to be assimilated to American society. Schools had to adapt once again to address the new challenges that faced them. Methods utilized were not always humane. Indian Boarding schools were ripe with abuse and the immigrants were subjected to extreme treatment to correct their attempt to communicate in their native tongue.

The turn of the 20th century brought a lot of change. As previously mentioned, child labor was still a contention. Now women began rebelling due to their experiences in the classroom. Some were displeased with the inability to move into administrative roles. "It was with that first class that I became aware that a teacher was subservient to a higher authority. I became increasingly aware of this subservience to an ever-growing number of authorities with each succeeding year, until there is danger today of becoming aware of little else." -- Marian Dogherty, Teacher, Boston, 1899 (Pinto, 2019).

The majority of teachers were women at this point, and their work was under constant scrutiny. They despised the control over them and wanted more autonomy, which was decreasing rapidly. Many teachers felt spied on and dictated to (Pinto, 2019). Poor pay and lack of benefits did little to alleviate the issues. Conditions were frequently deplorable, and teachers were given no real flexibility to adapt to the challenges in their student experiences. Overcrowding was common, poor students spoke little English, and classrooms were dirty and poorly ventilated (Pinto, 2019). The conditions were quite similar to those in the factories. Limited resources were a plight for the rural schools in addition to run-down buildings. Lack of funding was a constant issue.

Emphasis was on professionalism and City Boards of Education were seated by men who wanted reform that represented business professionalism. The goals of achievement and improving the teaching practice were admirable, but these men had no experience in a classroom. Business model efforts were used that included hierarchy, leaving teachers at the lowest level (Pinto, 2019). Uniformity and efficiency for classrooms containing 50 students were pressed on teachers, which also negated teacher initiatives as they were deemed too limited in knowledge.

Teacher rebellion ensued. Teacher's associations formed into unions. Two such unions continue to stand today: the American Federation of Teachers and the National Education Association. There is much to discuss regarding teachers' rights at this juncture, but little has changed since the turn of the 20th century in this regard. We can see the same fight for equal pay and autonomy in the classroom in 2019.

A new philosophy regarding education took flight in the early 1910's. Progressive education that took more focus on the experience and development of the individual child was beginning to be addressed. Today, we see branches of what began at that time when we look at schools of thought that brought about Montessori education, Waldorf education, and many more. "How can the child learn to be a free and responsible citizen when the teacher is bound?" -- John Dewey, Philosopher of Education, 1918. The focus of these schools was that if we remove autonomy from the teacher, we remove autonomy from the student. How can we achieve a free and democratic society if our population is being raised in such bondage? John Dewey demanded that democracy be embedded in the classroom so that democracy can flourish in society. What has transpired since his initial attempts to influence education has resulted in small branches of educators starting their own schools, independent from school districts, to accomplish such aims. These schools do not receive government funding and are frequently underfunded. Many rely upon the tuition provided by families who can afford it. This disproportionately leaves out those without financial means to attend schools that respect the whole child.

The 1950's brought about change in America, and this included the segregation of schools. Segregation was legalized in 1895 provided that the students received separate but equal education and facilities. Brown vs. the Board of Education of Topeka, Kansas in 1954 removed the segregation, and new levels of challenges arose. The segregated schools had been deemed unequal and that the Supreme Court agreed that desegregation needed to commence immediately. Busing was later addressed with Swan vs. Charlotte-Mecklenberg to ensure desegregation was supported through proper transportation in 1971. The 1960's launched more civil rights issues, community control over schools, as well as anti-poverty programs. Focus was also thrust upon Latino and Native American students. The continuous fight for the rights of students and teachers never ceased. By the 1980's, it was determined that schools were failing.

The "A Nation at Risk" Report in 1983 laid out the under-qualified teachers, underpaid teachers, poor working conditions, and poor student results (U.S. Department of Education, 1983). This was followed by "A Nation Prepared," which provided a guide for rehabilitating the education in the United States (Carnegie Corp., 1986). "This report argues that if the United States is to have a vibrant democracy, avert the growth of a permanent underclass, and have a high-wage economy, schools must graduate the vast majority of students with achievement levels long thought possible only for a privileged few" (Carnegie Corp., 1986, abstract). The National Board for Professional Teaching Standards was launched in 1987 as a result.

Education issues from 1990 to today are exactly the same as they have been since the inception of the one room schoolhouse and implementation of female teachers. Teachers remain underpaid. Class sizes remain too large. Conditions remain poor in many districts, especially those who serve minority or underprivileged communities. Additionally, teachers have had autonomy removed and even more standardization has been implemented. So much standardization took place after 2000 that nearly all classroom time was spent preparing for the numerous standardized tests required for schools to continue to receive government funding. Teacher performance based upon testing scores also dictated the stability of their employment. Schools have been sanctioned and many resorted to illegal activity to ensure their students achieved the desired results in order to maintain school funding (Chen, 2018).

> The call for uniform, high standards in teaching and learning has echoed throughout American history. Catharine Beecher and Horace Mann despaired of the low standards for teachers in the mid-19th century; 50 or 60 years later Progressive educators like John Dewey complained about ineffective teaching methods; all Americans worried about the state of our children's learning in the 1950s in the wake of the Russian rocket Sputnik, and in the 1980s we were convinced we were a "Nation At Risk" because of our low educational standards. With each outcry has come a new determination to define and implement better standards for our schools. (Pinto, 2019, para. 42)

With each new outcry, new pressures have befallen teachers and students alike, yet there have never been satisfactory results. The complaints remain the same, and the results unmoved. New efforts have focused on privatization of schools for better results, but they frequently use the same methods reinforced by other existing schools. Just a new pie with the same ingredients. Some ingenuity has come to fruition, but that often corresponds with technological developments, rather than teaching methods or school structures. One thing that has grown out of the pile of pressure is increased student behavior issues and attempts to control them.

~ 10 ~

THE PURPOSE BEHIND
BEHAVIORAL CONDITIONING

"The institutional role of the schools for the most part is just to train people for obedience and conformity, and to make them controllable and indoctrinated—and as long as the schools fulfill that role, they'll be supported." —Noam Chomsky, Understanding Power: The Indispensable Chomsky, 2002

Behavior

If one were to ask a school teacher or principal what is the primary focus area of their time at work, they would tell you that much of their time is spent on "classroom management" or behavior control. Most teachers tell you that they spend more time on behavior management than they do on lessons. Those who say they have great classroom management utilize tactics that often include removal of disruptive students or encouraging parents to medicate the child so that they can behave in class. Removal of students takes many forms. This frequently begins as a time out, detention, or being sent to the principal's office. More recently, new tactics such as isolation chambers are used to ensure that no one must deal with the child (Richards, Cohen, & Chavis, 2019). Students are basically sentenced to what would be the equivalent of solitary confinement in any prison. Solitary confinement has been found by many psychologists to be detrimental to the mental health of prisoners (Smith, 2006). However, teachers are encouraged to do what they need to do to ensure that classroom management remains strictly controlled.

Milgram

A famous study by social psychologist, Stanley Milgram, titled, "Obedience to Authority," demonstrated alarming results as to how willing people are to obey authority (Milgram, 1974). One could easily associate the behavioral conditioning performed in schools as the precursor to adults who will obey unwittingly despite the dangers posed. However, it is not isolated to the educational institutions themselves.

Schools reinforce this behavioral conditioning with the parents to ensure that it is continuous throughout the child's life. If the child only grew up with the consequences of disobeying authority, it would seem quite likely their tendency to defy authority would be greatly minimized. "As soon as the child emerges from the cocoon of family, he is transferred to an institutional system of authority, the school," where the student learns that "deference is the only appropriate and comfortable response to authority" (Milgram, 1973). Milgram states, "the modern industrial world forces individuals to submit to impersonal authorities, so that responses are made to abstract rank, indicated by an insignia, uniform or title" (Milgram, 1973). The ordering of compliance to authority regardless of legitimacy is reinforced within our education systems. This also increases the propensity for illegitimate authority to find itself in positions of government and employment leadership. A workforce and population of a nation can be easily manipulated if they have been conditioned to accept whatever authority has chosen to demand upon them.

Milgram was an active psychology professor at Yale University when he performed this experiment in 1963. His primary interest was in understanding why whole societies would comply with acts of genocide. Since his research, there have been countless demonstrations in numerous nations where the same behavior has been identified. In every instance, participants always stated that they were following orders (Milgram, 1963). In his research, the evidence supported that very few were willing to go against the orders of the authority figure. Most were willing to do the unthinkable even when it was clear that they were uncomfortable with it. Some did so without any acknowledgment of what they were doing. The basic result, people were likely to inflict harm upon another if they felt they were being watched and demanded upon by an authority figure. This did not even require aggressive demanding. No threats were issued. Basic statements to do the job were the extent of the orders given. Participants had also been told that they would be paid for their participation, but not told that their participation required obedience. Some were told they would still be paid if they left early when they hit their limit.

What were they asked to do? They were asked to give a test to someone in another room who was connected to electrical shock gear. The participant (called teacher) would ask the learner a question. If they answered incorrectly, they were given a shock. The shock voltage increased with each wrong answer. Teachers were also able to read the voltage warnings on the machine that they were to administer the voltage shocks from. The learner had also told them that he had heart issues, which set the stage for the teacher to feel compassion and concern for their well-being. The teacher could audibly hear screams by the learner as the electric shock voltage increased, although the learner was not actually being shocked.

A modern version of this test has been given by many different cultures and all have arrived at the same conclusion. This includes a recent version performed by ABC Television (USA) in 2007. Although the results were consistent across all versions of the experiment, there were factors that could have impacted the results. These include the fact that participants were volunteers, so potentially eager to please by nature. Smith and Bond (1998) point out that, apart from Jordan (Shanab & Yahya, 1978), most studies were performed in industrialized Western cultures. What this demonstrates is the consistency with compulsory education and willingness to obey authority since cultures with lack of education are less likely to be as conditioned to obey authority without questioning.

Although compelling, there were many variables that were not properly controlled in this experiment. Due to the volunteer nature of the study, there were no sufficient checks in place to generate an equal representation of different members of society. Although Milgram's sample was biased (all male), the newer examples of the same study did seem to identify these factors when attempting to perform more recent experiments of the same study.

There were additional limitations for the newer study due to changes in how experimentation on live human subjects can be performed. The result was still the same. One volunteer, a public school teacher who administered the test as the teacher role, proved to be the least likely to hesitate to administer additional voltage. She was the least bothered by the idea out of most of the participants as long as she could put responsibility on the authority for her actions (Borge, 2007). The results from this experiment are as follows:

- 18 men tested. 65% willingly administered increased painful electric shocks when ordered by an authority figure.
- 22 women tested. 73% willingly administered increased painful electric shocks when ordered by an authority figure.
- 30 were tested with an accomplice to guide them. 63% of them willingly administered painful electric shocks when ordered by an authority figure even when their accomplice urged them to stop.
- Subjects were educated as follows: 22.9% had some college; 40% had a bachelor's degree; and 20% had a master's degree.

Milgram's original experiment had fewer controls, but a larger sampling of 636 participants (Milgram, 1963). He also conducted 18 separate experiments across one region (New Haven) which he generalized as representative of an average American town (McLeod, 2007).

Ethics

The ethical issues with this experiment involved deception, however Milgram insisted that illusion is used to obtain natural responses to certain conditions otherwise difficult to obtain (Milgram, 1974). He did include interviews of the participants following the experiment to gather the effects of the deception on their psychological experience. 83.7% said they were happy to participate and only 1.3% wish they had never participated (Milgram, 1963).

Participants were exposed to extremely stressful scenarios. This is not something that is allowed in a lot of research performed today. The implications of psychological damage to participants is high. The distress of the participants was visibly noticeable (Milgram, 1963).

Symptoms also included trembling, stuttering, laughing, sweating, biting lips nervously, and digging fingernails into the palms of their hands (Milgram, 1963). Three participants had uncontrollable seizures (Milgram, 1963). Several pleaded to be dismissed during the experiment (Milgram, 1963). Milgram argues that these issues were short-term (Milgram, 1963). He also noted that their distress subsided when they were made aware that the person, they thought they were harming, was OK (Milgram, 1963). He did follow up with participants one year later to check if there was any long-term harm (Milgram, 1974).

Another ethical question was the right to withdrawal. Participants are to be made clear that they have the right to withdraw at any time during the experiment. In Milgram's experiment, they were encouraged to continue on numerous occasions. One could also say the same is true with students in the classroom. They are never given the choice to opt out. Commands given by the authority in the Milgram experiment said things like,

"Please continue"

"The experiment requires that you continue"

"It is absolutely essential that you continue"

"You have no other choice, you must go on"

Milgram's argument for these commands was to demonstrate obedience to authority (Milgram, 1974). In his defense, it seems rather clear that if the participants had been made aware, they have a choice, they would have been more likely to think independently. Classrooms across America do not encourage independent behavior. So, in this case, the correlation between Milgram's commands and what we see in our classrooms across America are valid demonstrations of conditioning to obey authority.

The legal and philosophic aspects of obedience are of enormous import, but they say very little about how most people behave in concrete situations. I set up a simple experiment at Yale University to test how much pain an ordinary citizen would inflict on another person simply because he was ordered to by an experimental scientist. Stark authority was pitted against the subjects' [participants'] strongest moral imperatives against hurting others, and, with the subjects' [participants'] ears ringing with the screams of the victims, authority won more often than not. The extreme willingness of adults to go to almost any lengths on the command of an authority constitutes the chief finding of the study and the fact most urgently demanding explanation. (Milgram, 1973, p. 62)

Milgram's Agency Theory (1974) explained the two states of behavior in which people will revert to in social situations. The first is the autonomous state. This is where people are in charge of directing their own actions, thus taking responsibility for their actions. The agentic state, which is where people allow others to direct their actions by passing off responsibility for the results of the actions. This enables them to do things they wouldn't do because it isn't their fault. For a person to enter the agentic state, they need to believe that the authority is qualified or legitimate and that the authority will accept responsibility for the results (Milgram, 1974). When Milgram told participants that they were responsible for their actions, most of them did not obey. Most refused to continue unless the authority was willing to take responsibility.

We can see similar behavior in the way that schools are now holding teachers responsible for the test results of their students. In turn, teachers are not only holding students responsible for learning the material, they are holding parents responsible for ensuring the students continue to learn outside of the classroom. The teachers were never given the option to not be responsible for the results of these tests. As a reaction, there have been many instances of illegal behaviors where teachers have helped students, or entire schools have falsified tests in order to pass strict demands that threaten to cut school funding and jobs (Thompson, 2018).

Attitudes About School

Some children thrive in a school environment. They enjoy the educational challenges presented to them. This can be a result of the teachers in the classroom, but often it is not. For myself, I was always reading. I began reading prior to entering kindergarten and teachers would have me help the other students who were learning to read when I was in first grade. By second grade, I wanted to read big books. My teacher would tell me I could not read such things, so I would check them out and read them anyway. This continued throughout my entire educational career. I was frequently challenged by teachers for reading things they did not believe I could read. Some would mock me. Some would look at me incredulously. I read anyway. This is how I passed the time when I was finished with my exam or classwork. I would read at any opportunity that I had. This was not derived from any motivation within the school walls, nor was it derived from home. Although, it was an escape.

For many children who are bright, reading is an escape from their environment. It affords them the opportunity to experience life from another's perspective. It is a window of information that may be severely limited in their immediate surroundings. Today, we have even more information available at our fingertips through the Internet. Book banning and Internet blocking are frequent challenges faced by students. In theory, it is to protect them from material that the adults deem inappropriate. However, not all material is truly harmful and sometimes this level of blocking also inhibits actual learning of material unrelated to the unrelenting block. It really is not much different than my experience with teachers who would roll their eyes or tell me I couldn't read something. When someone wants to learn, they will learn no matter what obstacles are put in their way. I know those teachers did not stop me.

There are various other attitudes about school which are commonly found in classrooms across America and likely in many other countries. Students are bored. Students are fearful. Students have anxiety. Students feel stress. School often represents something that many students dread going to everyday because they feel inadequate, they feel bullied, they are abused, or they do not feel challenged adequately. It is limiting from every angle. School is not a one size fits all scenario and it is not constructive for most students who attend.

Bruce E. Levine (2018) wrote in his book, "Resisting Illegitimate Authority," his own analysis in which conventional education systems punish impulses that are considered anti-authoritarian (independent thought) and reinforces obedience and conformity. Much like what Milgram also noted in his study on obedience. Levine's experience expressed his concern with why he had to raise his hand to go to the bathroom. How humiliating it was for some of the students with the way the teachers treated students who requested permission to go to the bathroom. He surmised that if a child had been shy, it would be quite likely they may simply wet themselves than to make a public acknowledgment of their need to use the restroom. That he felt some teachers were perverse in requiring a child to denote by finger what type of bathroom movement they needed to make (in front of the class). Then he commented on how disturbing many things in schools are, and that there are so many that we cannot possibly even think about all of them.

Victor and Mildred Geortzel (1962), a psychologist and educator, wrote Cradles of Eminence, a book that analyzed childhood experiences of 400 famous people. In this book, they surmised that the majority of them despised their school experience. This included the experience of Albert Einstein who went so far as asking a school doctor to give him a certificate stating that he had a nervous breakdown and must be dismissed from all class attendance. Einstein also purported that he believes that education through coercion and duty destroys the internal desire to see and search for answers. He felt that many of his teachers behaved more in alignment with military leaders than people encouraging learning. He was also noted to have failed his college entrance examinations on more than one occasion. He was told by a professor that he was impossible to teach because no one could tell him anything. Although I may have experienced similar treatment, I was talked down to about the way I wrote my own name by one professor. He proclaimed that I would not obtain a degree if I could not write my own name. I was working on a master's degree in another program while simultaneously working on a second bachelor's in computer information systems (his area). I only bothered to learn the things I needed to learn about computers and didn't worry about that degree. Degrees are trivial. If you have the skills, nobody cares if you have a piece of paper. I also have a name that even when typed, people somehow can't read. They are unable to see the name as what it is, they can only see a name that is familiar to them. His inability to read my name had much less to do with the way I wrote it than the fact that it went against what his mind wanted to see.

A recent nationwide study by Moeller, Brackett, Ivcevic, and White (2020) surveyed 21,678 U.S. high school students. These researchers, from the Yale Center for Emotional Intelligence and the Yale Child Study Center, noted a near 75% self-reporting of students surveyed experiencing negative feelings relating to school. They also noted that many of these students felt this way 60% of their entire day in school. Brackett noted that students looked at school as a place where they knew they would have a negative experience (Moeller et. al, 2020).

Modes of Coercion

Coercion is utilized in parenting, schooling, employment, and government agencies. This was not always the case. As discussed in previous chapters, children worked to help provide for the family before the compulsory education system was established, and for quite some time thereafter. Parents were not luring their children with trinkets, awards, or special treats if they would go to work to help provide for the family. Employers did not offer awards, trinkets, or special treats to motivate employees. What was most common at that time was abuse. Physical violence and psychological abuse. The most frequently used were threats to harm the person or their family. Employers went so far as to lock in the child employees to make sure they could not escape.

Physical violence has been utilized for centuries. Hitting or beating a child or slave was common practice to ensure that they obeyed or did what they were told. The fear of repeated physical violence was the motivation to not misbehave. It was an easy method because it did not require any kind of psychological understanding to correct the reason why the behavior was occurring to begin with. Sometimes the behavior was in direct response to the person feeling as if they were being taken advantage of or violated in some way. As such, abuse was used to quell the voice of the victim and prevent future outbursts or rebellion.

This is convenient for those who do not care about the experience of the person they are using to fulfill their needs. It is a means of control and domination. The other person is inconsequential, a means to an end. Some think they are protecting their child by abusing them to inflict fear in their mind for future memory recollection. Although it is a powerful way to trigger memory recollection, what it really does is create a trauma bond. After numerous instances or experience of trauma (either intentional or corrective) the responses developed ultimately render the victim disengaged from survival skills they need to survive future threats. What it does is create people who repeat the cycle of abuse either by perpetuation of victimhood to other abusers or by becoming abusers themselves.

Modern schools continue to use corporal punishment in some areas. Questionable controlling efforts were mentioned in the previous chapters. However, modern schools also offer a different approach. They utilize "rewards" to counter the punishments. This can be done through good grades. Other examples are rewards for recognition, special privileges, trinkets, or big prizes. The idea is that it is theoretically a positive motivation for the student to strive for something they want. On the surface, this appears preferable to threats.

There are numerous dangers to utilizing this type of coercion as well. The coercion through good grades encourages students to stop asking their own inquiries and to learn to obey and repeat what they are told. This method does quite the opposite of creating critical thinking skills to encourage a free and democratic society. It is creating a generation of people who won't question what they are told and future employees who will do as they are asked with menial tasks and not question the long-term implications of what they are being asked to do. This is probably one of the more dangerous facets of 'positive' motivation and coercion.

Another negative result from 'positive' coercion is competition to obtain the trinket. In theory, this would make the students strive to be their best to obtain the coveted prize. What competition often does is increase narcissistic tendencies to undercut, harm, or create a false scenario to win. This is the message many students receive, and it can be seen in our workplaces today. Narcissism is a significant problem in today's modern workplace and society. Even in our most recent modern historical event, we see people competing for toilet paper when there is literally no reason to panic shop. The mere suggestion of a threat prompts people to unthinkingly respond through illogical behavior that even resulted in a stabbing over something as menial as toilet paper. I was going to cite this, but after a quick search, I found pages and pages of incidents all from the same week across the globe, but especially in the United States, the United Kingdom, China, and Australia of this very behavior. It is truly shocking how widespread this really is. Google "stabbing over toilet paper" and find out more. What this tells me is that people are trained to respond dramatically to fear, and competition stirs their programmed motivation.

The area that has been clearly ignored in their educational experience is that of responsibility to others. Nowhere in our education system is that ever addressed. Instead, children are controlled to behave a certain way without ever being taught on how their actions impact others and how they have a responsibility to others. Not to the tune of sacrificing themselves for others, which ironically is exactly what narcissistic training teaches. Responsibility to others includes responsibility to self. This requires consideration of one's impact on others and themselves in making decisions. This is not something that is taught through coercion. Coercion is external, not internal motivation. So, when left on their own, they will not have the capacity for responsible internal motivation. I will get into this more later on.

Another challenge with these motivations is that children (or adults) only memorize long enough to pass the exam, but they do not retain the information. It is stored in their short-term memory. External coercion does not bring internalization of information. It triggers behavior, not motivation. It triggers reaction, not response. It trains people to respond to abuse favorably. Those who learn this well, become star trauma response fawners. They will do anything to avoid retaliation or to be humiliated or shamed. They will please anyone who they feel will impact their lives, regardless of how safe or healthy the situation is. Many will find themselves in abusive employment or personal relationships in direct response to this programming.

SALES ARE EASY. EDUCATING IS DIFFICULT. SALES INVOLVES TELLING PEOPLE WHAT THEY WANT TO HEAR. EDUCATING MEANS EXPOSING THEM TO THINGS THEY DON'T KNOW, AND HELPING THEM GET OVER THEMSELVES IN ORDER TO GROW. EDUCATORS CONFUSE SALES WITH EDUCATION. IF YOU HAVE TO SELL INFORMATION AND LURE THEIR INTRINSIC NARCISSISM IN ORDER TO ACHIEVE WHAT THE EDUCATOR THINKS IS THE GOAL, THEN YOU HAVE CREATED A MONSTER. EDUCATION IS NOT SOMETHING THAT ONE IS TOLD. EDUCATION IS SOMETHING THAT ONE EXPERIENCES. IN ORDER FOR THEM TO LEARN DEEPLY, THEY HAVE TO INTERNALIZE IT. PARENTS AND TEACHERS IN THE PAST HAVE OFTEN THOUGHT INTERNALIZING INFORMATION WAS DONE THROUGH THREATS AND REWARDS. PLAY WITH THEIR EMOTIONS TO FORCE MEMORIES. THIS IS TRAUMA TRAINING.

Other areas where this type of external coercion is harmful include one of the basic skills that schools, since their inception, have deemed a core requirement: reading. The National Assessment of Education Progress (NAEP) found that 64% of 4th grade and 66% of 8th grade students were reading at or below proficiency (NAEP, 2015). "These statistics are very troubling, particularly because reading below grade level in third grade is among the strongest predictors of later school dropout (Alexander, Entwisle, & Kabbini, 2001). Why would coercion in reading create such low scores? Shouldn't reinforced regular reading expectations improve scores? What key ingredient is missing to create such abysmal results?

Learning happens at various stages of life for everyone and not at the same time. Puberty does not happen for every person at the exact same age. Babies do not learn to walk or crawl at the exact same age. People do not die at the exact same age. Humans are biological creatures. Reading is a skill learned by biological creatures. Humans are not machines, thus not capable of developing skills at the exact same age. Pair this with external pressure, and for many, their motivation drops significantly. It feels stressful. It is unpleasant. If the child is not ready or slower than others, they become resentful and ashamed. The emotional factor involved with coerced reading takes a much larger toll on the results than any researcher has truly considered. For some, it becomes a traumatic experience, which will then trigger behavior patterns in relation to reading for most, if not the rest, of their lives.

The same could be said for learning math. It is well known how many people will loudly protest at the mere suggestion of knowing math and their experience learning it. Many have dismissed it as something too complicated or complex, so only a few really grasp it. Is that true? Perhaps for some, but it would seem much more likely that a broader percentage of those who studied math without coercion would likely retain it better having had the opportunity to study at their own pace and by choosing the method of learning that works best for their learning style or preference.

~ 11 ~

BEHAVIORAL CONDITIONING FOR SCHOOLS AND CAPITALISM

"The conscious and intelligent manipulation of the organized habits and opinions of the masses is an important element in democratic society. Those who manipulate this unseen mechanism of society constitute an invisible government which is the true ruling power of our country." Edward Bernays, Propaganda

Behavioral Conditioning in Schools

If coercion or external motivation is such a deterrent for learning, why do schools use it? Many would argue that they spend far more time with classroom management than they have time to teach various methods on how to read or do math (or any other subject). This has become such a focus that there are significant books and strategies encouraged by teachers and for teachers on how to manage classroom behavior. This is where behavioral conditioning in school becomes paramount.

Noam Chomsky has been known to speak on the topic of how the education system was "designed to turn independent farmers into disciplined factory workers" and that the society as a whole believes that:

> People are supposed to be passive and apathetic and doing what they are told by the responsible people who are in control. That's elite ideology across the political spectrum - from liberals to Leninists, it's essentially the same ideology: people are too stupid and ignorant to do things by themselves so for their own benefit we have to control them. (Kasenbacher, 2012, para. 11)

Additionally, schools track behavior records, and generate profiles on students which frequently label their behavior. This occasionally results in recommendations for medical intervention, such as drugging the child into compliance through medical approval. The sheer number of students medicated for behavior issues in American schools since the late 1990s's is staggering. Between 2011-2012, The National Center for Health Statistics reported that 7.5% of children in the United States between the ages of 6 and 17 were prescribed medication to control emotional or behavioral challenges (Howie, Pastor, & Lukacs, 2014). The number of children under the age of 18 that are prescribed psychostimulants increased six-fold to 4.2% from statistics taken between 1988-1994 and compared to 2007-2010 and that 1.3% of the children were prescribed antidepressants (National Center for Health Statistics, 2014).

What has resulted since the initial educational efforts of schools in the early 20th century has now become something which has been used through various media and social media platforms to manipulate behaviors of individuals throughout the world in order to create behavior patterns that fulfill the goals of the persons responsible for such campaigns. Cambridge Analytica is a perfect example of how tracking behavior patterns of individuals and collecting their data can be used to create very targeted campaigns to change their behavior and manipulate them to choose something they may not have otherwise. This includes choosing things that are not in their best interest or the best interest of the nation (Amer & Noujaim, 2019). At this juncture, any former protestation over the manipulation of minds for corporations has now been much more deeply transferred to the benefit of governments as well. This is additionally reinforced by school districts who force teachers to sign documents saying that they will never say anything against their government. This perhaps is intended to prevent teachers from inciting dangerous behaviors, but it also reinforces following what they are told, and reinforcing children to do what they are told. This is not the way in which democracy can function.

Over the last century, the world has seen numerous countries challenge the ruling classes. This resulted in revolutions that in many cases turned into dictatorships, communism, fascism, and other states where a vocal demagogue could easily persuade the masses to follow his lead in order to change the way that society has endured under the former leadership. In America, the increased exposure to schooling has directly correlated to decreases in challenging the ruling class. This was not the case in late 19th century America. Those with little or no schooling were able to organize trade unions, a large-scale working people's cooperative, and many other political movements that forever changed the trajectory of America including breaking the power of large banks in order for farmers to obtain easier credit (Levine, 2018).

John Taylor Gatto (1990) stated while accepting the New York City Teacher of the Year Award,

> The truth is that schools don't really teach anything except how to obey orders. This is a great mystery to me because thousands of humane, caring people work in schools as teachers and aids and administrators, but the abstract logic of the institution overwhelms their individual contributions. (Levine, 2018, p. 95)

Psychologist, Bruce E. Levine, has spoken extensively about these shifts in America and finds that schools teach compliance to hierarchy, obedience to authority devoid of actual respect, trains students to regurgitate information, socializes passivity in students and teachers, and for all to blindly adhere to reward and punishment systems implemented by authority figures (2018). One of the most concerning aspects he addresses is how people in our society currently pretend to care about things that are unimportant to them while simultaneously incapable of changing a life unsatisfying to them (Levine, 2018).

Jonathan Kozol, an educator and outspoken critic of the American education system excelled in his elite prep school career and later Harvard education. Kozol claims that children learn quickly that they will not succeed in school by expressing themselves, and that dissent must be channeled into polite discussion (Levine, 2018). Levine further highlights how Kozol states that institutions teach inert concern, which insinuates that caring is ethical by its own merits, but "disobedience is immature" (Levine, 2018).

It was previously mentioned that many nations that overthrew their governments were subsequently found to fall prey to communist dictatorships and fascism. This may also appear to align with what Noam Chomsky was referring to regarding people not knowing how to lead. There is truth to that as they have not had experience with leadership, nor had they received any formal or informal training on how leadership works. Former training was isolated to employment alone. There was no collaborative opportunity in their nations that offered any concept of democracy nor how to facilitate it effectively. The population was still programmed to be led and the most motivating voice that rose from the crowd drew their attention easily as they had already been trained to follow what appeared to be grand leaders from their former monarchies. None in the populace had any real experience with leadership and no knowledge on how to navigate a changing political landscape. Those who projected that they knew what to do easily persuaded the masses to believe them by telling them what they wanted to hear, regardless of their ability to fulfill those promises.

Much of the last century found many nations, including the United States, flooded with propaganda materials. The propaganda was designed to manipulate population behavior to support the goals of the government so that it could have more support than resistance to fulfill its numerous agendas. One such propaganda tool that emerged was the television. Just as the form of public schooling is content, so is the form of television broadcasting. Today, we would see the same in our online media and social network advertising exposure. Cambridge Analytica used our personal data to design propaganda designed to target individuals who were deemed persuadable to manipulate them in a particular direction to help facilitate political goals. This content was not necessarily factual. It was designed to invoke an emotional response as emotions tend to drive behavior. This is a conditioning process that utilizes the human trauma response to generate predictable behavior patterns.

Educational institutions are masters at engineering attitude and habit training. This is achieved through the structure and reinforced through punishments and award systems. Alexander Inglis wrote in his book (1918) "Principles of Secondary Education" that the purpose of education was to make people predictable in order for the economy to be rationalized. Make people predictable in order to accomplish this goal. Since humans are not predictable, the primary goal of school is to achieve this goal. Since he wrote this book in 1918, it has become obvious that the vain attempt to control human behavior is not so easily achieved. Schools have resorted to corporal punishment and the medication of children to reinforce this goal. If you were to ask any school administrator or teacher today, they would tell you that their number one issue is still classroom management. This will never change.

Darwin's "Descent of Man" motivated much of the decisions in the educational and business managerial systems when he stated that the overwhelming majority of human biology is fatally corrupted and cannot be improved because it is so far gone (1871). Much of what he wrote resulted in numerous atrocities in the last century such as locking up mentally ill persons, keeping them away from the remaining population so that they do not corrupt society. These gave many leaders the idea that they could manipulate the development of human improvement. This also resulted in breeding experiments and extermination of those who were deemed inferior in Nazi Germany (Spitz, 2005). In Nazi Germany and the United States, there were entire groups of people who were involuntarily sterilized so that they could not reproduce (Spitz, 2005; Wills, 2017). Many leaders were convinced they could achieve the perfection of the human race by taking measures into their own hands. The very first President of Stanford University, who held the position for 30 years, organized a class that would politically and intellectually take leadership over these decisions (Mendizza, 2009).

Darwin was not the first to address the ineptitude of man. John Calvin, French theologian, pastor and reformer in Geneva during the Protestant Reformation (1509-1564) stated, "that the damned are many times larger in number than the saved. The ratio is about twenty to one. There are too many damned to overwhelm with force, so you have to cloud their minds and set them into meaningless competitions with one another in ways that will eat up that energy" (Mendizza, 2009). In 1669, secular philosopher, Benedict Spinoza wrote that there were no damned or evil people because there was no supernatural world. He was more interested in the disproportion between those who have good sense, those who have what seems to be permanently irrational thinking, and those who are truly dangerous (Spinoza, 1669). He suggested an institutional school structure system as a 'civil religion' to eliminate formal religion, which he felt was irrational and dangerous, and to destroy the imagination of the irrational to prevent maximum damage (Spinoza, 1669). He also suggested that without this, people struggle against the chains and potentially cause local damage without doing fundamental structural harm since they cannot think beyond what they know (Spinoza, 1669).

As mentioned in a previous chapter, institutional schooling began in Prussia. In the early 1800s. Johann Gottlieb Frichte, a German philosopher, addressed the nation by explaining that Prussia's defeat with Napoleon was a direct result of soldiers taking decisions into their own hands instead of following orders (Frichte, 1808). His suggestion was that a national system of training would prevent those in the underclasses from imagining any other way to do things (Frichte, 1808). The very first institutional form of mass shooting occurred in 1820 (Mendizza, 2009). Class structure (social class) seemed rather fixed, according to Darwin (1871).

Behavioral psychologist, Wilhelm Wundt, began the first Institute for Experimental Psychology at the University of Leipzig in Germany in 1879. As we can see, the world now was ripe with change. Pairing the emerging study of psychology with the expansion of compulsory education would later lead to further experimentation on children and for the purpose of behavioral training and control.

Classical conditioning was the first of what would be many attempts to manipulate the learning process. Classical conditioning is most recognized as Pavlovian training, named for the psychologist who identified the way in which animals could be trained to respond to bells. Ivan Petrovitch Pavlov, a Russian psychologist, did his experiments on dogs in 1890. His first attempts were to measure salivation response in dogs when presented with food. He soon discovered that the salivation response would eventually occur because of hearing the scientist's footsteps in anticipation of the food that would soon arrive. The eventual realization was that dogs do not need to be trained to salivate. However, they can be conditioned to salivate through repetitive behavior triggers (Pavlov, 1926).

John B. Watson, behaviorist, believed that classical conditioning could explain all human behavior. He performed what is known as The Little Albert Experiment in 1920. In this experiment, a 9-month-old baby was exposed to various animals to set the normal response pattern that the child had no fear of animals. To condition the boy, a white rat was used. Every time the white rat was presented. Dr. Watson would make a very loud noise with a metal bar to scare the child. After numerous instances of this sound paired with the white rat presentation, the baby soon showed fear of the white rat with or without the sound (Watson & Rayner, 1920).

Burrhus Frederic Skinner would later take the front stage with his experiments that demonstrated programmed actions could be accomplished if the subject were trained through reward and punishment scenarios. Skinner differed from the classical conditioning behaviorists. He believed that humans also have a mind with more complex events worthy of study. He was more focused on looking at the cause of an action and what consequences resulted. His method was later called operant conditioning. Operant conditioning focused on how pleasant experiences in direct response to a behavior would encourage future continuation of the behavior, just as negative and unpleasant experiences in direct response to behavior would discourage future continuation of the behavior.

B. F. Skinner based his research on another behavioral psychologist, Edward L. Thorndike who determined learning theory at the Teachers College in 1898, which became the foundational focus for educational psychology. Thorndike identified that "responses that produce a satisfying effect in a particular situation become more likely to occur again in that situation, and responses that produce a discomforting effect become less likely to occur again in that situation" (Gray, 2011, p. 108–109). Tt is easy to see the way in which education evolved. It began with theologians and philosophers and was later to be adopted by psychologists and behaviorists. What has transpired since the behaviorists has only enhanced tactics that still support these psychological theories. There has been no further evolution in the psychology field to address education outside of the introduction of behavioral disorders and prescription medications to control behavior. This has resulted in even bigger profits for those who have their fingers dipped in the educational institution pot.

Private corporate foundations have been invested in the management of forced institutional schooling since the first Congressional Commission, called the Walsh Committee, in 1915. Justification for these actions was the goal of a utopian society and stable social order. Despite these goals over 100 years ago, forced educational schooling has failed to provide such results. In fact, they have produced behavior due to the escalation of mass shootings on a regular basis across the entire nation

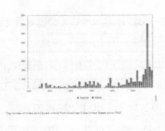

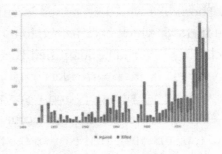

(Warburton, 2019)

Behavior Control Takes Precedence Over Learning

As previously mentioned, most teachers feel that classroom management takes a large portion of their efforts and time. Some feel they have things under control due to extremely strict protocols and institutional programs that are designed to remove disruptive students. Although attendance in school is compulsory, learning is not. It is encouraged through examinations, which are tied to government funding of schools. This motivates the administrators to pressure teachers to be efficient in their teaching and this has pressured instruction to teach to the test, rather than encourage genuine critical thinking skills. Yet, even with the most basic skill, literacy has fallen in recent decades to pre-20th century rates.

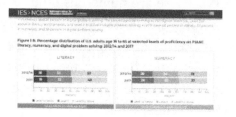

At the start of World War II (1939), literacy rates were found to be 97% of the adult population. When looking at the twenty-year survey of literacy rates in America, we can see that 20% of adults were illiterate in 1870. From that point forward, rates stayed similar, with a brief decrease followed by improving rates by 1979. High school also became more commonly pursued after World War II. This may have played a role in improved literacy rates. More years in school, improved textbooks, and more professionally trained educators played a role in improvements.

Efforts to improve education were successful. However, when we look at the most recent statistics of literacy rates in America, we see that these gains have taken a turn for the worse. This is after all of the major reforms in the 1980's, 1990's, No Child Left Behind, and the introduction of the Internet to the world. Access to information is clearly not a factor in decreased literacy rates. So, textbooks play no significant role since literally every type of information possible is available if one were to pursue it. This is far more information than what was available to anyone in the 1970's, let alone the 1940's.

Educational spending has increased substantially since the 1940's and 1970's, yet despite the effort to provide more support for learning, we do not see improvement. We see decreases in learning. The first angle of attack is to attack the teachers. Yet, today we find more and more school districts requiring teachers to be ever more educated. Many require master's degrees and continuing education classes to always stay current with the most recent strategies and trends. There are more education experts with doctorate degrees now than was ever available in the 1940's.

The only major change that began as early as the 1980s, and exploded from the 1990's on, was the use of pharmaceutical interventions to control behavior. This was not present before. That accounts for 9.4% of students nationwide diagnosed with Attention Deficit Disorder alone according to the Centers for Disease Control and Prevention. (CDC, 2019). There are numerous other diagnoses that can contribute to educational outcomes, including a very widely used diagnosis of Autism. Other interesting new diagnoses include things such as Oppositional Defiance Disorder. Most of these diagnoses will be described in medical textbooks as in relation to behavior, but especially as it pertains to classrooms.

Behavioral Conditioning for Capitalism

Why would we need behavior conditioning for schools? One would say to ensure students learn. However, it does not appear that this has been effective after the last century of educational reforms. We still have no progress. Perhaps there is something larger that this behavioral conditioning is designed for.

One could easily argue that this conditioning is preparing students for their future employment environments. This may have been true at some point, but as education has expanded, the purpose has become more and more muddled. Many justify the variety of subjects as exposing students to more for broader choice in their economic pursuits and employment options. Rare few truly specialize in the more complex subjects that are frequently required for high school graduation or college graduation. The higher the education, the more writing involved, and most of those degrees lead to professorships. As far as professional careers, the majority lead to teaching. There are experts in various fields who perform research independent of an educational institution, but they frequently work for government agencies or research laboratories funded by corporations who have specific goals in mind. This can also influence the research and lead to commercial sale of products not adequately tested as safe for public consumption. Despite the consumer protections in place, there are a lot of failed products that find themselves in our consumer market.

Pressure to deliver on a short time frame takes precedence over safety and quality in many industries. As students, we find children trained to perform under pressure with a finite deadline as well. The competition to perform above all others is the primary focus. Whether the personal best is attained seems almost secondary to winning above others. For those who are on the production side of corporate structure, they often do not find themselves with the freedom to be innovative. They are given instructions or orders and expected to follow-through. This can be under management that may or may not have better skills or knowledge than they do. There are many highly intelligent and skilled employees finding themselves incredibly hampered by their employment situation. They may attempt to do things on their own outside of the regular office hours, but they are limited with time and energy. This slows their development of new things, and sometimes dissuades them from pursuing anything at all. A rare few will push on no matter what. The system itself is designed to wear down employees so that they do not usurp their employers and design something better, thus becoming competition.

What this has done is create a world where the population would rather purchase from big name corporations than from their innovative friends or family. Innovators find that they usually have to seek support from complete strangers who see the skills and expertise separate from the person as an individual. We have created a society that dismisses the individual. The loyalty is to corporations and brands, not individuals. This results in people desiring to be employed by these big corporations. It is a status symbol.

Why would there be a need to reduce competition? Well, the market price is influenced by access to goods. If there is an overabundance of a certain type of product, the cost goes down and the profits decrease. Production must increase to meet demand. This results in more expenses for the corporation. It is less expensive to keep competition low, manufacture a limited number of items, and keep prices high so that demand is high. This decreases the corporation's overhead expense and increases profits for shareholders. This also reinforces brand recognition and brand loyalty, while also motivating the best in their fields to desire to work for these companies rather than start their own businesses. Lack of funding is often given as reason for this, but most simply do not have the stamina to endure what it takes to start a company and ensure it thrives.

Was this an innate issue or was this conditioned? After a minimum of 12 years of formal compulsory education that would not allow students to innovate or challenge the status quo, it is easier to see that they very well had it conditioned out of them to follow the leader rather than to lead. There are leadership opportunities within schools, but they are limited and skill specific. Absolutely none of them allow for governance of an entire institution or large peer group. What these leadership roles equate to are management, not leadership. How can they when the institution is also management and not leadership?

The way in which society is conditioned to follow orders serves the marketing efforts of these corporations. Language choices invoke emotions, suggest identity, and pressure decisions. In fact, these same sales scripts are often used in classroom teaching strategies and suggested to parents to be used with their children to motivate behavior. Everyone is being sold a script that is designed to manipulate decisions and behavior. Rather than providing all the information to make a logical decision, manipulative language is used to push the person to do what the salesperson, teacher, or parent wants. What this does is dismiss the intellectual faculties of the person being manipulated. When that person is not given opportunity to question what is being asked nor given opportunity to explore facts or options, the response from the manipulator is retaliatory in most cases. This is where guilt, shame, and projection come into play. Manipulation intended to make the receiver feel as if they are a bad person for not doing what they were told. Whether that is fact, is beside the point.

This is also how marketing has convinced consumers to purchase things they do not need. This has resulted in the manufacture of millions of items that are not only unnecessary and frequently unused, but it also fills our landfills and pollutes the earth in ways that are literally destroying our environments. Those who question this are treated as traitors and dismissed as villains. All of this fits the narcissistic abuse cycle.

Student Resistance

Since behavior management is the primary focus of educators world-wide, there must be a reason for the behavior. Why would children need to be controlled? What are they doing that needs to be controlled? Why would they behave this way? What motivates their behavior? Ironically, these questions are never asked by school administrators or educators. There is a blanket assumption that children are inherently bad and that they need to be trained to behave as civilized members of society. This is reinforced with parents so that there is a unified front on this attempt. It is so extreme, that pressure to put children in school at younger and younger ages is seen as an achievement and guarantee of success.

Parents are willing to pay large sums of money to have their children placed in schools as early as possible. Why would parents be so eager to put their beloved children in the hands of strangers when they are quite young? They have been manipulated to believe that their child will fail in life if they do not receive the best education possible as early as possible. As if there is a ticking time bomb above their child's head that says they are too late if they don't do these things as quickly as possible. Parents become quite competitive over this. It's almost as if getting one's child in a school early is a sign of competitive success. They win. They achieved the goal that was challenged before them. They do not even question why.

Children go through separation anxiety because it is unnatural to separate a child from its mother at a young age. It is such a common issue that there are books and numerous resources to help parents expedite the process so that the educators (or childcare workers) can move forward with the tasks at hand with no further disruption. The sooner the child no longer needs the parent, the more convenient for the educator. No one questions what is best for the child and they certainly don't ask the child what they want. They are irrelevant.

Younger and younger children are finding themselves diagnosed with the previously mentioned behavior disorders and recommended prescription drugs to facilitate the educator's efforts with less disruption. No one asks why the child might be disruptive. That child's experience is irrelevant.

As the child matures, they find that this way they are always dismissed becomes so aggravating that they begin to cause much bigger problems both at school and at home. Again, no one asks why the child might feel this way. The child's experience is irrelevant. It must be handled and taken care of so that the adults can continue with their plans for the child.

Some children eventually give in and stop arguing. At this juncture, the teachers and parents are pleased that the child has succumbed to the expectations and no longer questions why or whether it is OK that they are experiencing these things. They just do what they are told and get it done to move on to what they do want for themselves. Some parents allow the children freedom of choice in that, others do not. Some parents have children so over-scheduled that they become psychologically depressed and withdrawn. At this point, the child no longer wants to talk about it because they already know that no one will hear them no matter what they say. They realize their cage.

There are parents who are abusive and educators who are abusive. This is another level of issue that plays a role. However, the abuse is always tied to the narcissistic abuse cycle and thus quite easy to predict and manage when those in charge are aware and can make protections for the child to no longer be subjected to the treatment. However, the system itself also uses the narcissistic abuse cycle to function. So, the child may only find themselves removed from the more dangerous version only to be left within the same cage, but less terrifying. This is easier to accept if the child can accept that it is safe. Most of them do not. Therefore, they will not trust the adults who attempt to help them. They know that the whole situation is just another layer of the same thing. They know they will not be listened to and will never be given agency over their experience. Their need to survive will always take precedence over the need to please adults. The more the adults control them, the more the child will become destructive in response to the trauma they feel they cannot escape.

~ 12 ~

MODERN SCHOOLING

"Little children love the world. That is why they are so good at learning about it. For it is love, not tricks and techniques of thought, that lies at the heart of all true learning. Can we bring ourselves to let children learn and grow through that love?" John Holt

Introduction

Many teachers and administrators in public, charter, and private schools feel that they must control children in order to ensure a constructive learning environment. Teachers and administrators do not trust children. They do not trust students to make decisions about their own learning. They do not trust students to help teach one another. They do not trust students to learn on their own.

I have witnessed many teachers in schools recoil at the notion. Their number one issue is classroom management. Classroom management currently dictates a large portion of school time. Stopping the children from behaving in ways that prevent learning or "waste time." The pressure to perform a certain level by a certain time is very real for the teachers, who then put this on the students. The teachers are pressured by the school district and the testing mechanisms put in place to make sure everyone learns certain things by a certain period of time regardless of their abilities, cognitive challenges, personal challenges, and speed in which they learn. The student is the product rather than the focus of the learning environment.

Behavior Management

As a result, there are various strategies that have been used in many schools to curtail and prevent behavior issues. These can range from time out, having their desk moved to another part of the room away from their peers, detention, or loss of recess. In extreme cases, the student may be placed in in-school suspension, external suspension, or even expulsion. Some schools even resort to isolation chambers. The challenge with these actions is that attending school is compulsory, so they are literally putting the student out of compliance with their own government's compulsory attendance laws. The primary focus is to put fear in the student, so they give in and comply. It has much more to do with the convenience of the adults in achieving the objectives than it is about understanding why the child may be reacting the way that they are.

Some schools implement awards systems to motivate good behavior. Utilizing operant conditioning methods derived by B.F. Skinner. Children have been conditioned through training methods to respond on command. I have witnessed teachers use clapping, whistles, songs, and other trigger sounds to achieve these command responses. The orders received in the classroom are frequently:

Sit down

Line up

Pencils down

No talking

Raise your hand

Go to the bathroom on permission

Eat when we tell you to

Do not skip school

> Do not leave early without external justification provided by an authority

Rewards are then offered to children to achieve these tasks consistently. They are lauded as high achievers and dutiful citizens. They are given special prizes, privileges, and public acknowledgment. These manipulative ploys are using the brain's reward system to attempt to manipulate behavior. The brain's reward system is designed for survival. It is not designed for use by external parties for manipulation and control. To do so is rewiring the brain development of the child permanently. This is also found in those who threaten victims in domestic abuse. The mechanism is the same. Programmed hypervigilance is achieved.

Students are often discouraged from reflection. Teachers will publicly shame a student for staring out of the window or for not looking at the lesson being taught on the board. There are many things that could have been occurring in the child's mind during that time. The child could have been thinking about an experience they had that their mind is attempting to resolve or find a solution to. They could be envisioning something they wish to write about or create. They could even be contemplating the lesson being offered at that exact moment in time. Maybe something the teacher said rang something meaningful in their mind and they are truly grasping the concept on an even deeper level than the teacher offered. All these reasons are valid brain processing responses to stimulation and brain development. To have a teacher interrupt this process disconnects the development that had been occurring.

Educational Gains Not Met

Perhaps we would feel more confident that education was truly serving a public good if the education outcomes and gains promised were achieved. However, this is simply not the case. The purpose of education is not and never has been improvement of educational skills. None of the research studies that have addressed the efforts used to support the testing machine have been taken seriously unless they supported testing. In fact, there is no grant funding for research that doesn't support the sales of some kind of educational material. Anything that supports human interaction changing between adults and students is blatantly ignored by grant funding unless they can support the manufacture of a product to support this change. Despite this, the basic educational skill proficiency of students in the United States is bleak:

> The assessment shows roughly one-third (34 percent) of U.S. eighth-graders and 40 percent of fourth-graders showed proficiency in reading and math in 2017 -- a trend that's remained since a jump in scores in the 1990s and early 2000s. In the last report in 2015, that figure was 25 percent for 12th graders. (Farland, 2018. Para. 5)

There is currently no evidence that the non-stop efforts to reform education, as previously mentioned in other chapters, have failed. Gimmicks are utilized and entertainment efforts engaged to lure children's interest. It is failing. What it has done is teach adults how to be manipulative through efforts that condition children for narcissistic abuse with absolutely no evidence of educational attainment at the end of the effort. This is abuse.

Cultural Identity

There is much discussion over the theoretical white washing of education in America. This is not accurate. Education is not directed for any culture in America. In fact, it has removed every culture from its curriculum. Therefore, we see a lot of our white population with resistance and fear over other white populations worldwide. It isn't exclusive to those of color. Those of color are easier to identify visually, but those who hold on to their cultural identities are attacked vehemently.

This is not a mistake. It was intentional since the inception of compulsory education. The removal of all cultural identities and the formation of holidays unique to America were formed in a vain attempt to create a unified population. This has been a profound failure. This also ties deeply into epigenetic trauma and ancestral roots that will not allow a population to forget where they come from. The only response left is hatred for those who still demonstrate healthy expression of their culture or denial of one's own roots. As if we are orphans from any ancestry. There is a huge disconnect in identity when this occurs, and schools have exacerbated this wound with their curriculum enormously.

Our current education model began in China. It was there long before it made its way to Prussia and beyond. The United States of America only pushed it in the last 170 years. To know what the education system is designed to do; one needs to look at the countries who had it first. As we can see, America is next in line for a communist state. Yes, this is the point of the system. It was never put in place to liberate citizens. It was put in place to replace slave labor or to condition the slave labor in specific directions. They put tinsel on it to get people to comply, while simultaneously making it compulsory and illegal to not participate. Propaganda is spread to make the population reinforce this belief so that independent thought is not allowed. Media is controlled. Entertainment is controlled. Loyalty is to the state first, employer second, and family last. A compliant workforce must be weak.

Tribal culture values strength and integrity. Protection of the clan. Not what we have in America. Countries with unified cultural populations can incorporate their cultural ancestry as part of their education. This means that America will never achieve this goal as it is a melting pot nation. To attempt to remove cultures entirely is genocide of identity. To try to create a unified identity violates epigenetic identity. It cannot be done, and it will present in cultural clashes for centuries. This cannot be removed from human identity.

Study tribal cultures and the way they interact. It is evident that it is a critical component to their entire existence. It is not something they study under a microscope and analyze. The result of colonization was the separation from the core human components, making everything systematically separated and controlled. In order to accomplish this, reinforcement of cultural identity denial is absolutely required. It is all around us in the U.S.A., and it is intentional. To deny one's roots and the core values of one's ancestral people, makes one dependent upon the information they are being fed to lead them. The lack of core identity found in the U.S.A. is painfully obvious and has exacerbated our abusive tendencies. Abuses that are directly in correlation with not accepting one's stripping of identity.

Oppression

This brings us to the oppression that is inherent in this type of an educational system. To oppress identity and create a uniform population that will serve their employers, it is important to keep them from focusing on what they resonate with. They cannot be tempted to find things that are counter to the end goal of a compliant workforce willing to accept conditions that may not be in their best interest. They push awards and possessions as goals to motivate the students and the workforce.

> The oppressors do not perceive their monopoly on having more as a privilege which dehumanizes others and themselves. They cannot see that, in the egoistic pursuit of having as a possessing class, they suffocate in their own possessions and no longer are; they merely have. For them, having more is an inalienable right, a right they acquired through their own "effort," with their "courage to take risks." If others do not have more, it is because they are incompetent and lazy, and worst of all is their unjustifiable ingratitude towards the "generous gestures" of the dominant class. Precisely because they are "ungrateful" and "envious," the oppressed are regarded as potential enemies who must be watched. (Freire, 1970, p. 59)

To appease angry parents who are dissatisfied with the schools, there have been recent attempts to launch "charter" schools that are theoretically more in tune to the children and their individual interests. However, in practice, they are not really any different from the schools the children left. They may have better facilities. The expectations remain the same. Many of these schools are heavily supported through philanthropic investment from those who wish to have their own influence on education.

The largest issue with philanthropy today is that the government is excluded from solving the problem and the government is society (democratic society). So, by circumventing this, philanthropists are pushing personal agendas forward through contributions that ultimately benefit them in the end. Charter schools are a perfect example of how wealthy are using government funds to support their own financial coffers under the guise of providing improved education. There is no accountability and the families are misled in believing that they are gaining an improved education for their children.

This is not to say that public schools were healthy nor providing what is needed. The issue is that no one is doing what is healthy or needed for children. The entire structure is about education jobs, curriculum development profits, and more. The education industry is one of the largest employers in America. It is a cash cow. People will not do anything to change the cash flow for those profiting from what is going on. If anything, they are exploiting a government required attendance policy to ensure a captive consumer which guarantees profits for them for many years.

> "The Rockefellers and others funded research at the University of Iowa Child Welfare Research Station in the 1940s that tried to show that it was children's home environment, not their heredity, that determines their success. They proved that if you changed the environment around children — gave them better toys, better ways to play, and such — that you have better outcomes. That was controversial proof that you could intervene in a poor child's life, that their poverty was not a determinative factor." Anand Giridharadas (Lindsey, 2018, para. 27)

Although charter schools began in the last 20 years, it is evident that interest in the education industry has been in full force since the 1940's. This was also around the same time that efforts to increase education enrollment beyond eighth grade also began to expand. The longer we keep children in school, the longer we can profit from the educational industry. With students forced into attendance at least until they reach 16 years of age, and some through 18 years of age, we have even more products to design and more people to employ.

The implementation of student loans in 1965 has seen an ever-increasing push for students of every educational capability pushed to attend college and take out loans to attend. The banking industry became heavily invested in education as a result. It is so extreme that the current student loan debt held by borrowers in America exceeds $1.7 trillion dollars. This does not guarantee that degrees were awarded. Debt is owed whether the education is completed. Those with higher levels of personal challenges to overcome can sometimes find themselves in debt and without a degree. Thus, making their situation even worse than it was had they never gone to college in the first place.

It goes beyond cultural oppression and financial oppression. It also includes intellectual oppression. Noam Chomsky has written quite extensively on how education in America is used to suppress intellectual development and encouragement from those who could make meaningful changes to the status quo.

> In fact, the whole educational and professional training system is a very elaborate filter, which just weeds out people who are too independent, and who think for themselves, and who don't know how to be submissive, and so on—because they're dysfunctional to the institutions. (Chomsky, 2002, p. 111)

Not only does it limit intellectual curiosity in students, it also holds parents hostage to what they can do with their own children. Classroom rules are finding their way into family homes and the society. The school's demands keep the parents jumping to the beat issued by teachers and school administrators. Family time is no longer family time. It is the parent's turn to keep educating the child for the school's goals. Reinforcement of adherence to this can be easily found when a parent tries to remove their child from the school to pursue home education. It does not matter if the parent feels that the school inadequately addresses their child's education needs, requirements to obey the school district's demands remain (McDonald, 2018).

For those whose children have never fared well in a traditional classroom setting, attempts to utilize individual education plans theoretically designed with parents and teachers together, are limited to the school's resources and understanding of how to do it. Most schools are woefully equipped to educate children of varying intellectual capacities and handicaps. This includes gifted children. Parents who have removed their children from school in order to meet their children's individual education needs have often found themselves the target of a child-protection investigation utilized by the school district in order to bend the will of parents to comply with the school (Klein & Preston, 2018). The schools' vested interest isn't in the child. It is in the number of heads they can count in their funding allotment. More heads mean more money.

Many of the families who find themselves strong-armed are incapable of taking legal action due to their economic limitations (Klein & Preston, 2018).. Those who come from wealthier families will rarely see this type of action taken by a school. Poorer families have come to expect it as a normal process for them. The school district and city government have no fear of financial retribution by the parents who cannot afford to take such legal actions against them. Whether the parents are following school regulations at home or not does not stop these attempts to pursue education neglect actions against parents (McDonald, 2018).

> If, as Chomsky suggests, many of us have grown acquiescent to power due to our successful schooling, it can be hard to challenge authority. It can be even harder when that authority is strengthened by government force and when we may not have the resources to fight it." (McDonald, 2018, para. 12)

Expectations

Expectations for children have also changed dramatically in the last generation. Students are expected to learn at younger and younger ages, despite research that says such efforts are harmful (Carlsson-Page, McLaughlin, & Almon, 2015). Pressure to perform begins as early as kindergarten. Only thirty percent of teachers had reading expectations for kindergarten students in 1998. By 2010, that number rose to eighty percent of teachers not only expecting reading in kindergarten, but to become proficient readers that same year (McDonald, 2018). Not only does this show disregard for the developing brain at this age, it also incorporates emotional psychological programming of inadequacy, anxiety, and confusion (Carlsson-Page, McLaughlin, & Almon, 2015).

The pressure to encourage parents to put their children in childcare that incorporates learning skills at younger and younger ages is also disconcerting. Due to the lack of family nurturing time and the high ratio of children per adult, these developing minds are being wired to feel more insecure than those who are raised with a higher number of adults per child in a familiar home environment. These younger years are critical brain development years and they should not be handed over to strangers for development. The most critical development that can occur at such young ages is social-emotional development, fine motor skills, and establishing their place in a family unit. These fundamental factors are not properly addressed in any school setting or childcare facility as the structure is the reverse of a family unit and no adult is going to have the same level of investment in that child's emotional development the way that a family would. This eventually leads to disruptive behaviors in the elementary grades and beyond.

Drugging Children

The drugging of children for behavioral compliance and management has become common in America. Since schools have never been questioned as the source of contention, the answers sought have always been how to correct the student to fit the school's demands and needs. The advent of stimulant medication that demonstrated the ability to alter child behavior in a classroom setting became incredibly focused upon in the 1990s and beyond. The ramifications of such medication on a developing brain had never been studied. The results in the classroom were what determined the medication successful despite the potential risks and side effects. Many parents found themselves bullied by schools and childcare facilities to have their children labeled as hyperactive or oppositional so that they could be adequately medicated to make the job of the teacher easier. This was deemed more effective than the punitive strategies utilized to remove the child from the classroom for the benefit of the other students. Not once has the child's experience been a consideration.

The U.S. Centers for Disease Control and Prevention (CDC) reports that approximately 11 percent of children ages four to seventeen have been diagnosed with ADHD, and that number increased 42 percent from 2003-2004 to 2011-2012, with a majority of those diagnosed placed on medication. Perhaps more troubling, one-third of these diagnoses occur in children under age six (McDonald, 2018).

As we place children in classrooms and childcare facilities at younger and younger ages, we see steep increases in diagnosis of hyperactivity and attention deficit. Oppositional behavior has also been noted. This is especially true for those who have parents who work long hours and are not able to spend as much time with their children each day. The family connection essential to their young developing minds is ignored and replaced with structured facilities that expect the child to adapt to a group rather than learn to understand its identity within a group as would be done in a family unit. The craving for attention and feeling nurtured is not something that should be diagnosed and drugged. Not to mention that some of these children are demonstrating trauma responses. Their "bad" behavior is the only way they know how to cope with what they are experiencing. The response to this behavior is more aggression and detachment (fear and abandonment), which only reinforces the trauma for the child. This is in addition to the expectations in schools that the child may or may not be adequately developmentally ready for.

"Mindfulness"

Another popular trend is to utilize a concept called "mindfulness" to address children's behavior in classes. There is a new national movement focusing on "Trauma Informed Schools." While in theory, this should be considered a good thing considering the stress many students are facing every day in their classrooms. Even more critically, schools are not fully aware of the traumas students experience outside of their walls. There can be abuse in many forms taking place in their homes, neighborhoods, or even within the school itself. Although it is supposed to be the school's responsibility to monitor behavior and prevent abuse within its coffers, it frequently fails to accomplish this task. School shootings have been on the rise since the late 1990's. Now, it is so common, no one is surprised anymore. Schools initially started closing campuses and hiring security or police to remain on campus during school hours. Now, many states are arming the teachers.

One thing that these mindfulness attempts miss is that traumatized students are vigilant for a reason. This is an instinctive protection against future trauma. To tell someone who has been severely traumatized that they are safe and that their mind is wrong creates severe cognitive dissonance that can wreak havoc on their functionality. They may lash out (fight), stop communicating and resist instruction (freeze), leave the class and refuse to return (flight), or become overly helpful in the attempt to gain approval (fawn). All of these are trauma responses and one cannot simply tell a developing brain that they can forget what their brain has taught them to survive because the class is doing it. It is also truly detrimental for the students who face bullying in school. They know they must remain vigilant to protect themselves. They can never feel calm and safe until they know they are safe.

Mindfulness can be powerfully effective in the context of overall healing (Mallon, 2019). The classroom is not a counseling center, a licensed therapist, or psychologist. Teachers have no business implementing therapeutic tools without training on the entire psychological impact that this may have. This brings to question: how many roles must a teacher play? Security guard, police officer, mother, therapist, psychologist, teacher, and the list goes on. The bigger question is: would it be so bad to change schools so that it is not so painful and difficult for everyone? This is not representative of a constructive learning or teaching environment. It is indicative of an organization that has a big goal and they do not care what it takes to get there, even if there are serious losses and damages in the process. This is irresponsible management and it should not be allowed.

I am heartened that the phrase trauma-informed has entered the public consciousness. It serves as a guard against seeing mindfulness as a quick fix to complex problems. Some educators who promote mindfulness in schools are speaking caution about the fact that even closing one's eyes feels dangerous to some children—along with offering guidelines about how to teach it safely. Currently, California's Surgeon General is bringing attention to the fact that Adverse Childhood Experiences lead to poor health outcomes later in life. The point isn't to make everyone so self-conscious about trauma triggers that we stop taking risks in helping others. The point is to bring the culture in line with reality. Techniques do not heal people. But techniques, skillfully applied, can be powerful tools for healing. Trauma survivors are uniquely positioned to teach others what really works for them (Mallon, 2019).

Trauma is caused by the sheer removal of a child from his or her home at a young age to be educated and pressured to perform much sooner than their developmental capacity can allow. The tactics used by teachers and administrators to reinforce behavior management and conditioning further exacerbates trauma that any child has endured outside of the classroom and within the school itself. The blatant disregard for their developing minds to meet expectations and goals for those financially benefiting from their educational experience is criminal.

Lack of Interest

We also cannot ignore the student's own interest in receiving education in the manner they are forced to receive it. Students are frequently described as showing no interest in education. It has become so commonly observed that researchers did a study to find out how students felt about school. What they found, across all demographic groups, was that negative feelings are prevalent and included feeling tired, stressed, and bored (Moeller et al., 2020). This does not negate positive experiences in school, but the prevalence is concerning as education does not occur when these experiences are normalized. For effective learning to occur, students need to feel interested or curious at the very least. Engagement is predictive of deeper and more enduring learning (Moeller, 2020).

If the students are not learning, they are not interested in learning in this format, and they are experiencing trauma in the attempt to educate them, then what are we doing? It is being done for the benefit of adults, but the children will also eventually become adults. What kind of society do we create with this effort? The rise in psychological illness in the adult population in recent decades is an alarming statistic that we are not only harming our children, but our future adult population who will be governing our populace and providing care and services to those who rely upon them for their efforts. What kind of society are we creating? Is this worth it?

~ 13 ~

COMMON PARENTING PRACTICES

Parenting

Most parents have the best intentions for their children. Many are nervous about making mistakes and this frequently encourages them to seek the best possible solutions to help them raise responsible and productive people. This has also resulted in the production of a multitude of parenting advice books, videos, and all manner of tools to help parents learn the best and hottest new approaches to parenting.

Parenting is treated almost like a fad. The only things that have remained consistent over the decades are the ways in which abuse is normalized in parenting. This includes the way parents speak of their children in front of them or behind their backs. This includes controlling their children in ways that disempower their children, but make the parent look strong in the eyes of strangers. This includes reward and punishment cycles so frequently purported by schools as the best gimmick to manipulate behavior the way parents desire. It also includes physical and emotional abuse and manipulation.

Normalized abuse occurs in the way parents speak of their children. Many parents have referred to their children as jerks, annoying, or even extreme names like assholes. Parents expect other adults to laugh with them and agree. If the adults who witness this do not agree, the parent who uttered the original words may lash out at the disapproving adult or peddle their way out of their statement to save face. The action of calling anyone a name or describing who they are as a derogatory description is abuse. The way some parents talk about their child's behavior, suggesting that the child must need medication or a therapist rather than asking the child how they feel about what is going on, is a red flag. Many do not include the child in how the family functions. In many respects, parenting is frequently remarkably similar to a hostage situation. Children with no voice are very frequently treated as hostages. The 'do as I say,' 'too bad,' 'well that's the way it is' parenting - is hostage parenting.

Parents who disempower their children by controlling them for the benefit of others do so by aggressively speaking, yelling, grabbing their child in front of others, or shaming them. They also disempower by speaking in ways that reinforce obedience, rather than discussing with the child their needs and choices. These are parents more concerned about how they appear in front of other parents than they are of the impact they have on their child's experience. The need to have perfectly behaved children is reinforced by society. Parents are shamed by other parents for not having obedient children who do not act according to adult standards of behavior. In this sense, the society disempowers the child and sends a message that they are not good enough to be included in their experience.

The reward and punishment cycles are also utilized in schools. In most families, they involve charts for chores, and rewards such as activities, trinkets, or food. This can include academic performance as well as household chore accomplishment. The problem with this cycle is that it teaches the child that these activities aren't important unless you have a reward for accomplishing them. The purpose of the chore or the academic performance is lost on the award promised at the end. This is carrot on a stick dangling abuse. It is so common, that there are major industries supporting this type of reinforcement by educators, schools, psychologists, and companies who sell items to use for this type of behavior modification. The message of why is lost in the entire process. The ownership over the activity is completely lost. It is obedience to an external party with a promise of reward if completed. This ultimately reinforces the potential for predatory people to prey upon the child because they have already been programmed to respond to this type of treatment.

Other major parenting manipulation tactics include physical punishment and verbal shaming. As previously discussed, public humiliation, shaming, and language used to instill guilt feed the fear mechanism and it signals to the brain to protect itself. The child will ultimately learn sneaky behavior to avoid additional experiences like this. The shame component can last into adulthood and manifest in all numbers of maladaptive behaviors that impact social connections, relationships, and employment capacities. Physical punishment such as spanking or slapping does the same type of trauma trigger in the brain. The signal tells the brain to avoid the person causing the harm, so the logic learned is not a rational choice to not do the activity again. The lesson learned is that the person doing the behavior is unsafe. The child will do whatever they intend to do but do it in a manner that hides it from the person who inflicts physical pain on them. This also includes verbal abuse, such as yelling.

Socially Reinforced Narcissistic Parenting

Our society only congratulates women for what their children are doing. They ignore women who excel professionally or academically overall. On social media, you see clear evidence of this. Women who post pictures of their children get tons of likes and hearts. Those who post things about their business doing well meet a lot of crickets. They may get a few likes, but overall, the response is non-existent. We reinforce women needing attention through their children. This forces women to expect things from their children that are emotionally and developmentally inappropriate. We turn the children into performing monkeys for the women who are performing for a society that won't let them be fully functioning adults in society. The string is from the society itself. Women who opt to go outside of this norm and be a successful businesswoman and a mother are often shamed unless they post a lot of proof that their children are doing amazing things. There is a need for society to see the product under construction properly displayed like a meal being prepared. The children are not heard, and they are often treated harshly if they do not operate according to the parents' need for attention.

This can also be true for fathers/men, but women bear the brunt of this. Often, they may be doing it for the abusive/narcissistic male whom they are married to, had children with, or are dating. It is rarely about the children. The children are the fodder for the accolades craved. When you remove this from the equation, women find themselves socially isolated for not playing the game as instructed.

State Allegiance Over Family

The indoctrination through compulsory education removed children from their families. This was more severely done with the Native

Americans. It was initially done to strip them of their cultural heritage and knowledge. America is a melting pot of different nations, so there is no common thread. School has served a bigger purpose with not just industrial revolution workforce needs, but also with the removal of loyalty to family over loyalty to the larger state. The way in which courses that focus on any cultural heritage have been banned or watered down reinforces the efforts by the initial boarding schools to strip the various cultures of their heritage and knowledge. More importantly, we have now trained parents to feel that their children need to go, or they will live miserable and dire lives. We have added certification requirements for jobs that can be done without a piece of paper proving skills. By reinforcing the certification process, we reinforce taking the child away from the family unit and their heritage to go to an external school that controls what they learn.

To see how this has truly played out, look at the way parents think raising their children is a job to complete before sending them out of the house. The parents are not loyal to the children. They treat the children as an obligation they had to fill for the state (society). They were all too eager to wash their hands of the children after the children reached 18 years of age. What the state wants is the focus. The failure to look at the children's future as cohesive with their own long-term survival needs is short-sighted. Many tribal cultures and cultures around the world still operate in multi-generational family units. The whole family unit takes care of each other, which provides stability and loyalty to the family.

Most cultures who are not broken are remarkably close with their family relations. Not just 'visit on holidays' close. They take care of their family regardless of age. Family support is ongoing, but not in the manner that enables laziness. Laziness is the fear of American-style nuclear families that they will be 'taking care of' adult children past 18. They are petrified of such notions. The reason for this is that they were trained to parent in a manner that is unnatural.

Many Boomer children were raised with grandparents in the home with their parents. The Boomers were the first generation that found an economic shift in the country that afforded them the ability to have separate homes from their parents. The Great New Deal, launched after the recession of the Great Depression, set them up to have a level of financial security never achieved in America. This also encouraged the one income home. However, as more women wanted to join the workforce, increases in family disruption occurred. Prior generations had grandparents who could provide childcare. Boomers frequently left their children to fend for themselves after school. Daycares were not common and babysitters often young and unprofessional. The Boomers were the first generation to experience large numbers of divorces and individual adult focus. Focus on the children was last. Children were at the mercy of whatever the parents were doing. Most of the time, those parents didn't care or notice what their children were doing.

Helicopter parenting came as a boomerang effect from negligent parental behavior that found so many abuses occurring to children. Now, we have parents who don't allow their children to develop because they are overly doted on to the extent that they are breeding a new class of narcissist. The kind that needs enablers. The kind that cannot stand on their own. They will be parasitic for their survival. Whether that parasitic nature comes from them demanding the government take better care of them or if they choose to do it on a significant other, remains to be seen. However, we are seeing more and more demands for the government to take care of people.

Women fought to have the right to work. Women wanted to have independence from abusive spouses. This is a real complaint and a valid argument. Women needed the ability to sustain themselves in order to get out of an abusive situation and protect their children. To this day, this is still a challenge as the cost of everything has truly prevented one-person earnings providing for an entire family. This is in direct correlation to women working. Keeping women in lesser paying jobs or paying them less for equal work reinforces it further. Families are not supportive of divorced mothers and tend to make them fend for themselves. This has much to do with the belief that the parents are no longer deeply connected with the grown child. They are now accountable to the state. So, if they help, they are helping the state. It's not about the reality of the adult child. It is not even about the reality of the grandchild.

One indirect correlation with the introduction of compulsory education was the gradual lost family bond that ensured survival of the family. Instead, children are taught to seek validation outside of that. Look at what compulsory education has done to families. Now older people miss friends who die as they age and have no solid relationship with their grown children. Abuse in families is bad. Abuse by society to force families into sterile relationships by name is worse.

Control vs Self-Control

The need to control others derives from lack of self-control. Many do not know how. Since the compulsory school attendance laws reinforced school attendance, and schools reinforced children learn to obey orders by outside parties, self-control is never fully developed. Utilization of the previously mentioned parenting strategies also reinforces children to do what they are told without fully understanding why. This creates populations who will follow orders despite the harm they may be causing or the long-term impact of what they are being told to do. The reinforcement of reward and punishment cycles guarantees mindless obedience. Without external controls, many find themselves behaving recklessly and mindlessly. As a result, you see so many trying to control their surroundings. It is 100% lack of self-control. Children lack self-control. So, they are controlled. If they never learn self-control, they learn to control others. The root is fear of no control. Feeling some sense of control either externally or internally reinforces the feeling of safety, which is fundamental to survival. When survival becomes reliant upon external control, abuses occur, and the cycle continues with no recovery without a full disruption of the systems and parenting practices that reinforce this pattern.

Reward and Punishment Cycle

The reward and punishment cycle is supported by many parents, schools, and child psychologists as the best way to manipulate your child to choose behaviors you want from them. This can include performing tasks or accomplishing goals. This programming system rewards the brain for meeting the goals and sends signals to the brain that this is something to continue. It does not tell the brain whether what they accomplished was truly good for them or if they should question why they are doing it. It teaches them to do as they are asked, and they will be rewarded for making that choice. This is a tactic used by many abusers to lure their victims into doing things that go against their own safety or well-being. By electing to use this cycle, parents are inadvertently teaching their children how to appease an abuser. They are also making them less inclined to question what is asked of them in other environments (peer pressure) or future employment. The goal is to create eager employees willing to do what is necessary to meet the organization's goals. Unfortunately, not all organizations are ethical and not all unethical behavior is transparently exposed to all employees. The reward cycle truly sets our children up to fall for predatory behavior that can harm their long-term health and survival.

On the opposite side of this system, the punishment cycle is intended to teach children to not repeat behaviors or actions that are undesirable. In theory, this would appear to be constructive. However, based upon the way the brain develops, it trains the brain to avoid the person who will implement the punishment. It does not deter the behavior as much as the strategy the child will choose to do it. Additionally, abusers use punishment to incite fear in their victims. This generates a trauma bond when the abuser vacillates between loving and fearful behavior. The entire reward and punishment cycle is in line with abuse training of children. It should be avoided at all costs.

Additionally, punishments escalate conflict and shut down learning. They elicit a fight or flight response, sending the frontal lobe's sophisticated learning capacity into basic defense response. The emotional response will consist of any number of maladaptive emotional responses such as guilt, shame, anger, or oppression. These emotions are used by abusers to control their victims. Oppression does not happen by accident. It is systemic and widely utilized in America to control various levels of our population to go against our own best interests to appease a larger entity that uses people to meet their own agendas. If an organization was supportive of its people, it would not need to cause psychological damage to its staff in order to accomplish its goals. There are many organizations beginning to utilize servant leadership styles and other more democratically fashioned functionality in order to foster a growth mindset in the entire staff, propelling the organization forward more effectively and cohesively. There is no reason for education systems to utilize a method that trains the students to obey without questioning or without having a voice. Parenting needs to prevent this from becoming the norm for children.

People who were trained to take instruction from outside of themselves and promised reward have been found to be slower at solving problems. The adult population demonstrates this every day. Many will wait to be instructed on what to do and they often will not do anything unless given some external reward for choosing to do what is asked. Rewards become the focus and the brain isn't used to its fullest capacity as a result. Deep thinking, reflecting, and seeking various possibilities are tossed aside for the reward promised instruction option. The Milgram experiment reinforced this.

Additionally, this cycle reinforces the belief that children need to be controlled and manipulated by adults. This supports the assumption that children do not have innate good intentions without this manipulation and control. If children were spoken to in powerful ways that reinforce their capability and capacity for empathy, we would find a larger response demonstrating cooperation, hard work, and collaboration. The children can make sound decisions when given the space to develop their own sincerity. Parents who demonstrate empathy and an eagerness to hear their children also show their children what that looks like so that they can learn from experiencing it.

Behaviors Developed as a Result of Parenting

One of the largest obstacles facing children is the same as what is facing their mothers. American mothers face high levels of shaming from many sources regardless of how well they are raising their children. This is a major sign of narcissistic abuse by society toward mothers. This is then passed down to the children by the way in which the mothers feel they are pressured to behave with their children. The results are often smothering, fearful, aggressive, and lack deeper connection that is necessary for healthy relationship development. This also explains why so many teenagers rebel against their mothers.

This can also lead to mothers being more concerned about how they appear to others than how they connect with their children. This is narcissistic parenting. It is not exclusive to mothers. Fathers have also used children to harm the mother of their children when it suits them. There are many divorce courts loaded with examples of this type of behavior. The entire dynamic is unhealthy for children. The way in which society manipulates women using their children to control them is abuse.

This can also impact the emotional regulation of the parents within the home. When parents are challenged in other areas of their lives, they can sometimes communicate aggressively and callously with their children. Waller and colleagues (2018) found that lack of parental warmth and harsh home environments lead to the development of callous and unemotional behavior in children. It would be possible to compare this type of environment to that experienced by the Romanian children in the orphanage mentioned earlier in this book. Perhaps not quite as drastically, but in some cases it may be similar. Not all parents are warm and loving. Many were not raised in warm and loving environments, so they continue to pass this behavior on to their children and the cycle continues.

Another common behavior is that of parents trying to please the school to demonstrate that they are a good parent. This has been found to be problematic in some homes especially during periods of grade reporting to demonstrate academic achievement. In one study, "nearly a 4-fold increase in the incidence rate of verified child physical abuse reports was found on Saturdays after a Friday report card release" (Bright et al., 2019, p. 176). This decreased if the report cards were sent home earlier in the week (Bright et al., 2019). This does not mean that there were no incidents, however.

Parental Controls Backfire

Many parents believe they must control their child's consumption of technology, media, and other personal choices. Many parents feel that this is an ongoing struggle in their homes and they often find their children sneaking the forbidden activities. As a result, many parents will put their children in numerous activities to keep their children busy. Rather than having the child engaged in something they genuinely enjoy; they are externally reinforcing activities the child may or may not be interested in. This also creates a lot of stress for the family not just in interpersonal relationships, but also in financial obligations, and time commitments. In coordination with the frequently used reward and punishment cycle, technology, media, fun activities, and food are frequently used as rewards to encourage compliance. Tang et al. (2018) found that in order to decrease the child's personal screen time, the parents had to do the same. To deny the child the same freedom sends the brain a threat message, which inadvertently inspires the child's behavior to go behind the rules of the home for them to have the same freedom as their parents. It would be far more effective for the family to have a discussion on appropriate use and the types of things they will expose themselves to so that the family is respectful of all users throughout the home. This will encourage the child to communicate their interests with the parents where discussions can naturally occur, and resistance does not become the normal behavior in respect to healthy boundaries.

Dehumanization of Children

The generalized treatment of children in American society is dehumanizing. Children are basically at the mercy of adults to be granted permission to be human. They must get permission to cry, to go to the bathroom, to have a say over their own bodies, to have emotions, or to have struggles. Children are not granted permission to have personal boundaries against adults in their lives. This varies from parents, to relatives, all the way to childcare workers and teachers. The adults have determined who has rights to the child, but the child is not given the authority to make their own boundaries on what they are comfortable with.

The way in which children are spoken to is very dehumanizing. Adults have the authority to be impatient, rude, and demanding of the child, but the child does not have the right to do the same with the adult. Adults minimize the child's experience and feelings and no child can do the same with any adult. Adults can threaten a child with physical violence, emotional abuse, abandonment of affection, and the loss or destruction of their property, but no child can do the same with an adult. Adults can bark orders at a child, but no child can speak to an adult that way. Adults can disrespect a child in any manner they choose, but a child is not allowed to disrespect an adult.

Much of what is done to children is the opposite of preparing them for adulthood. It prepares them for abuse. It truncates their emotional development and ensures that adult relationships will be rife with strife and difficulty. Without having a secure and mutually respectful relationship with adults, children grow up to not know how to have mutually respectful relationships with anyone. This can cause all manner of difficulties in their personal relationships as well as their working relationships. It also makes them more vulnerable to predatory people who will harm them.

The dehumanization of children is called childism. Childism is a prejudice or discrimination against the young. It is also a systemic condition that promotes stereotypical beliefs about the young. The way in which parents are rewarded for dehumanizing their children in our society is part of our overall oppression issues in our nation. To raise children believing that they do not deserve to be respected, to have the authority over their own minds, bodies, feelings, and intellect, raises a population that will follow leadership that will utilize the same dehumanizing behaviors to control vulnerable populations. This is further reinforced by the way adults mock, shame, publicly humiliate, blame, and victimize their children in order to win favor with fellow adults. Narcissistic parenting breeds mental illness in children. This is supported by our society and its systems. There are areas of progress being made, but they are far from adequate. Most often, parents who elect to be more respectful of their children are ridiculed and attacked by parents who support narcissistic or authoritarian parenting behaviors. This is the nature of the narcissistic abuse cycle.

~ 14 ~

THE ALTERNATIVES

Creative Collaborative Environments

In this chapter I will criticize the competitive emphasis that exists in current schools such as letter grading, standardized tests, etc., in contrast with more natural approaches such as experiential learning, student leadership, and intrinsic motivation. First and foremost, "the teacher cannot be the only expert in the classroom. To deny students their own expert knowledge is to disempower them" (Delpit, 2006, pp. 32-33). Jacobs reinforces and adds that "ultimately, most studies conclude that transformative learning is most apt to occur when courage is associated with any and all aspects of being, thinking, doing, and believing" (Jacobs, 1998, p. 169). In order to obtain such transformative learning within the classroom, the teacher must allow the students to participate in the teaching and exploring of material or ideas, even if it means that the students may find their original thoughts incorrect upon completion of the discovery period. The opportunity to participate as a teacher also reinforces the learning for the student who teaches. Another aspect to consider is the environment. Students need a supportive environment which enables them to freely express who they are, while simultaneously enabling them to engage in the responsibility of their learning experiences. If the classroom offers support and life exploration without coercion, the students will naturally grow with a sense of responsibility (Harrison, 2002).

Some teachers have experimented with different approaches in their mainstream classrooms. Researchers such as Philips have spent considerable time on Native American lands, observing, and listening to the interactions of the students in the classroom as well as in their tribal community. She describes how students respond when given the ability to control their own educational process.

> The Indian student verbal participation in group projects was not only much greater than in either whole-class or small-groups encounters, but also qualitatively different. As a rule, one could not determine who had been appointed as leaders of the Indian groups on the basis of the organization of interaction, and when the students were asked to pick a leader, they usually ignored the instructions and got on with the task at hand. In essence, they transformed the group-project organizational format so that it could no longer even be said to be a variant of the small-group participant structure. There was never any conflict over who should be directing activity or over who should be carrying out what task. Suggestions were either ignored or supported verbally and carried out. The students worked quickly and effectively and completed their tasks without intervention from the teacher. They often turned the activity into a competition between the groups, verbalizing their desire to finish what they were doing ahead of the other groups (Philips, 1983, pp. 119-120).

She then contrasted their behavior to those of their Anglo-Saxon counterparts. The behavior was strikingly different. The Anglo children would attempt to identify a leader quickly, who then would control interactions with the other students. Students often disagreed with approaches to the task, and leaders were challenged with administering their authority. This behavior resulted in the teacher's involvement to resolve disputes. The students did not complete the tasks in the allotted time and did not engage in the same type of competition as their Native American counterparts did (Philips, 1983).

Community Based Education

Another observation found by many researchers is that non-Western educational traditions utilize communal or community focused learning. They do not identify educational specialists (teachers). Education is deemed a social responsibility of the entire community. If their culture did utilize formal educational structures, the instructors did not receive formal training (Reagan, 2005). Indigenous education relies on unity to inspire a self-realized potential that intertwines with the community, the self, and humanity's place in the world (Mezerow, 1991).

There are numerous varieties of community-based education that also work in conjunction with collaborative learning environment philosophies. Many of these describe themselves as democratic or learner-focused schools. Students are given options for classes they can take or suggest classes they would like to have. If they can bring together enough students interested in the subject, then a teacher chosen by the students who also agrees to teach the class, will create the student-generated class. Once they commit to the class, they have to complete it. They chose it. They created it. They must finish it. If the student cannot find others to join them, they can pursue the topic on their own and find a mentor in the school who is willing to work with them on their studies. There are no limitations to student learning focus and the focus is frequently encompassing numerous subjects simultaneously, so it is a whole-curriculum type of learning experience, rather than a segmented learning experience. This helps the student to thoroughly understand the concepts and be able to apply them to real world situations.

Grades are not frequently given in such schools. If they are required by the government to issue grades, they frequently will issue them solely for the government, and give the students and parents the option to see these grades. They have found that by giving grades, the students are less motivated and become less cooperative with their fellow classmates. One could easily say grades also incite narcissistic behavior. Students who feel inadequate may try to manipulate the teacher or fellow students to make themselves feel more powerful to make up for their feelings of failure. That is not to say that failure is not a helpful learning experience. It is more impactive through failure in action rather than a piece of paper with a letter. Failure in action offers an immediate opportunity to assess the issues in real time, analyze for possible solutions, and the chance to correct the issue immediately. This is not punitive, but immersive learning in real time.

These schools also infrequently use testing. Testing is used only as the students and the teacher feel it is necessary to ensure learning, but often, learning is demonstrated through the daily efforts and interactions among students as well as the teacher. Since there is no competitive hierarchy to prove one knows more than others, the entire group (who chose this class and may have arranged it) are invested in the entire learning process and facilitate it collaboratively.

Anyone who misunderstands something will be identified throughout the process and aided by peers or the teacher at the moment of discovery to help them to understand. This does not have to involve the entire class. It could be a student peer helping the student, or it could be the teacher. They can even do this outside of class time and often it is done during their more communal activities. There is no limitation to learning time and no limit to methodology.

Governance

Students were also charged with the management of student behavior. The teachers and administrators participate, but this democratic environment ensures that everyone has a voice and is heard. This is where our original student councils derived from. These schools hold what they frequently call "meetings." If there were issues that day or week, they would bring the issue before the school in a meeting to discuss the problem, and everyone can suggest solutions. After all options are heard, they vote on a group decision. The decision is then implemented. This means that school rules are voted on by the students and teachers combined. Students are more inclined to follow their own rules because they also chose them. If they violate them, they must face their peers as well as the adults to have the group meeting to decide what should be done. It has been found that students are more humane to their fellow classmates than traditional schools are with their punitive measures. As a result, students do not continue to behave poorly. Classroom behavior and classroom management is not a real issue.

While it goes without saying that not all Native American tribes are or were the same and this is likewise true for all the African tribes, I choose to focus generically on these two cultures because broadly speaking, both come from a more chronologically recent tribal living standard, both tribal cultures utilized generally similar educational methods, and both have statistically scored lower on standardized examinations than their Asian and Caucasian counterparts (National Assessment of Educational Progress data, 2007). In these respects, they are similar.

Tribal Concepts

I will first discuss what the general aspects of indigenous education were for both the Native American people and the African, then go on to cover in some detail the role that epigenetics may be playing in Native Americans' and African Americans' success (or lack thereof) in the Western-style education system, then finally conclude with a potential solution to this challenge which suits these cultures' epigenetic and historic traditions while encouraging their highest self-expression in our modern society.

Another term that has been used in light of the experience of Native American cultures is "ethnostress." Ethnostress, as defined by Cajete, "is primarily a result of a psychological response pattern that stems from the disruption of a cultural life and belief system that one cares about deeply" (Cajete, 1999, p. 190). This disruption and creation of ethnostress occurs quickly yet continues to be transmitted through future generations. Although one might be able to notice the effects immediately, the long-term effects can vary and impact future generations' perceptions of their own self-image and their understanding of their culture's global identity and place in the world (Tribal Sovereignty Associates, The Power Within People, 1986).

Pre-Colonial Learning

Compulsory education began in the 1850's with the primary focus of providing much-needed factory workers for the budding industrial revolution (Gatto, 1992). One exception to this purpose was the boarding schools which were created to remove the Native American children from their tribes, and who's primary intent was to "Kill the Indian in him and save the man" - Captain Richard H. Pratt (Adams, 1995, p. 52). Freire elsewhere points out that violence has never been initiated by the oppressed. Rather, the violence is initiated by the oppression itself (Freire, 1970, p. 55). More specifically, those initiators of the compulsory education laws and boarding schools did so to force change upon all cultures. The aim was to create a unified nation with one cultural identity.

Prior to colonization, these societies had a common method in educating their youth. They utilized oral tradition, a communal approach to childhood education, and non-formal educational experiences (Reagan, 2005). Another reason I chose to focus on the two generalized tribal cultures of Africans and Native American people is that these two groups were both imposed upon by Western colonization. Africans were uprooted from their native land and shipped to North America while the Native American peoples had their land, way of life, and culture taken away by the European colonists who displaced them in North America. Both received significant life-threatening shocks to their prior existence. This shock manifestly included their educational practices. I will first discuss African culture before European slave raids.

Pre-Colonial Africans

Pre-Colonial Africans, broadly speaking, utilized four major types of political organizations: stateless societies, chiefdoms, kingdoms, and empires (Ayittey, 1991). The most unlike our Western approach is the stateless society. These stateless societies were intended to prevent autocracy and tyranny. With no "authority figure" representing the tribe, communal governance flourished (Ayittey,1991). These stateless societies were instinctively democratic in nature (Williams, 1987). This statelessness brought about a natural evolution of democracy. It was therefore in the societies without chiefs or kings, where African democracy was born and where the concept that the people are sovereign was as natural as breathing. Therefore, in traditional Africa, the rights of the individual never come before the rights of the community. These self-governing people did not have a utopian society in any idealistic sense. Theirs was a practical society in every way. Their laws were natural laws, and order and justice prevailed because the society could not otherwise survive. Theirs was not a theory, but a government by the people and it was a government for the people (Williams, 1987).

It would become obvious then that education in traditional Africa would prepare the children to live in such a society. Everything that the child was taught involved socialization in the material and spiritual sense, taught the child to think collectively, and progressed with the natural development of the child as they matured (Moumouni, 1968). The effectiveness of this education was possible because of its close relationship with life. It was through social acts (production) and social relationships (family life and group activities) that the education of the child or adolescent took place, so that he was instructed and educated simultaneously. To the extent that a child learned everywhere and all the time, instead of learning in circumstances determined in advance as to place and time, outside of the productive and social world, he was truly in the "school of life," in the most concrete and real sense (Moumouni, 1968).

Another educational component that reserved high importance in many African tribes was the development of character in children. Fafunwa identified this as "the corner-stone of African education" (Fafunwa, 1974, p. 21). "Sociability, integrity, honesty, courage, solidarity, endurance, ethics and above all the concept of honor are, among others, the moral qualities constantly demanded, examined, judged and sanctioned, in ways which depend on the intellectual level and capacities of the child and adolescent" (Moumouni, 1968, p. 22). Okeke stated similar sentiments in his writing on "Traditional Education in Igboland". In his writing, he emphasized sociability, truthfulness, bravery, stamina, the ability to maintain humility and irreproachable conduct was of such importance that all members of the community would take it upon themselves to address the child (praise or correction) as necessary. There was no separation of responsibility in the rearing of children. (Okeke, 1982)

Education in Africa was not separated from living. Just as the political structure was communal, so was the educational approach. Education was very inter-personally collaborative and connected very closely with the natural and spiritual life of the community. The implementation and focus of education were characteristically multivalent. Progress was gradual and conformed with the child's physical, emotional, and mental development (Moumouni, 1968). Education had to be practical and germane to actual life in the community. In "pre-colonial settings, such education was generally highly effective" (Reagan, 2005, p. 62).

What made this type of education effective? The entire focus of the lessons was imminently practical and therefore applied directly to the child's life, even to their and their tribe's very survival. There was an immediate and obvious purpose to it. The children learned everywhere all the time. This culture, therefore, could be said to embrace whole life learning.

> The story the Leavers have been enacting here (earth) for the past three million years isn't a story of conquest and rule. Enacting it doesn't give them power. Enacting it gives them lives that are satisfying and meaningful to them. This is what you'll find if you go among them. They're not seething with discontent and rebellion, not incessantly wrangling over what should be allowed and what forbidden, not forever accusing each other of not living the right way, not living in terror of each other, not going crazy because their lives seem empty and pointless, not having to stupefy themselves with drugs to get through the days, not inventing a new religion every week to give them something to hold on to, not forever searching for something to do or something to believe in that will make their lives worth living. And - I repeat - this is not because they live so close to nature or have no formal government or because they're innately noble. This is simply because they're enacting a story that works well for people - a story that worked well for three million years and that still works well where the Takers haven't yet managed to stamp it out (Quinn, 1992, pp.147-148).

Daniel Quinn's Ishmael describes Leavers as the indigenous cultures and the Takers as the "civilized" society. This theme is found frequently in many Hollywood films and numerous stories.

Pre-Colonial North Americans

Like African political structure, Native American cultures also tended to be what we now call democratic. For example, the Iroquois Indians are known to have used a democratic system. In fact, this system is what the United States' founding fathers utilized to create the democratic governmental structure that we have today. "Although each tribe had leaders, they did not have control over the population but acted instead in accordance with the wishes of the tribe" (Caskey, Rapida, Wubbold, 2001).

Education in Native American cultures encompassed the complete person which meant awareness of a mind, a body, and a spirit. The goal was not merely to acquire specific skills, but to learn how to be a complete human being. The belief systems were very deeply imbued with spirituality, meaning every physical thing was endowed with a spiritual component. It was believed that a person's mind, body, and spirit must be in harmony in order to have wellness. Without this harmony, it was thought that anything learned could be used to hurt others. "Knowledge without the spiritual core is a very dangerous thing" (Forbes, 1979, p. 11). Another important factor is that each person was also considered to be their own teacher and so the lessons learned were connected to individual life experience (as with the African approach) (Cajete, 1999).

What made this type of education effective? Students learned how to become self-reliant, independent, aware, and connected to their community. It was education for living that addressed each aspect of the person. Skills were more easily acquired because the student was harmonized in his or her body, mind, and spirit. Native American cultures, therefore, also embraced whole life learning.

Native American and African students came from different yet similar educational belief systems prior to this colonization. In the

Native American cultures, students learned how to become self-reliant, independent, aware, and connected to their community. It was education for living that addressed each aspect of the person. Skills were more easily acquired because the student was harmonized in his or her body, mind, and spirit (Cajete, 1994; Reagan, 2005). Native American cultures, therefore, embraced whole life learning. The African child's lessons were imminently practical and therefore applied directly to the child's life, even their and their tribes' very survival. There was an immediate and obvious purpose to it (Reagan, 2005). The children learned everywhere all the time. This culture, therefore, could be said to embrace whole life learning as well. Both cultures had immediate purpose and application to their education. Upon subjection to the Westernized educational systems, they no longer had immediate purpose and application to their education. This is a cultural shock to their historically natural learning styles and methods.

The Western mechanistic separation-oriented way of teaching, learning, and living is very contrary to what the African and Native American cultures were all about prior to colonization. It is no surprise that they would have difficulty adapting to something so completely foreign to their historically successful way of understanding and living life. What is more fascinating to me, is that their holistic way of living and learning is perfectly aligned with the new concepts recently discovered with the realization of quantum physics.

European settlers had dismissed the Africans' and Native American peoples' way of living and understanding as something antiquated that would delay progress. This very Newtonian view of the world propelled by Western schools is now being proven drastically incomplete and has contributed greatly to the physical destruction of our planet (Kornblith, 1997). The product of such schools are students who do not see the whole picture. They are so narrowly focused on specific subject concentration that they do not realize the implications of these efforts on other important areas of life. Indigenous education relies on unity to inspire a self-realized potential that intertwines with the community, the self, and humanity's place in the world (Mezerow, 1991).

Oppression

African and Native American children were initially forced into colonized or Western-style educational institutions starting in the mid-1800's. Some were completely removed from their families and cultures. Native American children were forced to speak English, cut their hair, wear western-style clothing, and punished for speaking their native tongue. "Only by attending boarding school could Indian youth, stripped bare of their tribal heritage, take to heart the inspiring lessons of white civilization. The educational solution to the Indian problem appeared to be at hand" (Adams, 1995, p. 59). This initial exposure to Western-style educational institutions, not to mention the genocide described by Guenter Lewey, could easily have created a traumatic enough experience to affect future generations and their abilities or desires to resist conforming to Westernized education.

> Thus, according to Ward Churchill, a Professor of Ethnic Studies at the University of Colorado, the reduction of the North American Indian population from an estimated 12 million in 1500 to barely 237,000 in 1900 represents a "vast genocide . . . , the most sustained on record." By the end of the 19th century, writes David E. Stannard, a historian at the University of Hawaii, Na-

tive Americans had undergone the "worst human holocaust the world had ever witnessed, roaring across two
continents non-stop for four centuries and consuming
the lives of countless tens of millions of people." In the
judgment of Lenore A. Stiffarm and Phil Lane, Jr., "there
can be no more monumental example of sustained genocide—certainly none involving a 'race' of people as broad
and complex as this—anywhere in the annals of human
history." (Lewey, 2004, para. 3)

John Holt alluded to the notion that some children were intentionally withholding their intelligence and abilities from their rulers
(teachers, etc.) to declare their minds free of their enslaved bodies
(Holt, 1964). Perhaps some students do intentionally withhold their
full capacity from the educational institutions that demand their attendance. I believe, however, that with the emergence of epigenetics
research, it will be found that these students are unconsciously resisting the authoritarian school model due to epigenetic pain memory. I also feel that they are resisting this Western-style educational
format out of sheer subconscious survival instinct. Freire states that:

> The oppressors do not perceive their monopoly on hav-
> ing more as a privilege which dehumanizes others and
> themselves. They cannot see that, in the egoistic pursuit
> of having as a possessing class, they suffocate in their
> own possessions and no longer are; they merely have.
> For them, having more is an inalienable right, a right
> they acquired through their own "effort," with their
> "courage to take risks." If others do not have more, it
> is because they are incompetent and lazy, and worst of
> all is their unjustifiable ingratitude towards the "gener-

ous gestures" of the dominant class. Precisely because they are "ungrateful" and "envious," the oppressed are regarded as potential enemies who must be watched (Freire, 1970, p. 59).

I agree with Freire's view on oppressed peoples and so believe that it is possible that the African and Native American peoples (students) are instinctively resisting the education that was created by their Western oppressors in America. They somehow know deep down that it is detrimental to their own survival to succumb to this hierarchical structure which intentionally kept their people oppressed for generations.

Tribal Culture

All peoples come from tribes. In America, the general population primarily identifies Native Americans as the only tribal people. This is a direct result of compulsory education in America. The influx of immigrants around the turn of the 20th century brought an increased pressure on schools to unify instruction. Simultaneously, the effort to "kill the Indian and save the man" meant that the eradication of tribal culture in America was also to be abolished. The purveyors of education may have vainly attempted to create a unified nation by removing all people's tribal identity to create one narrative. This includes all the European tribes as well.

It is easy to see how effective this has been with the White population in America. Most may have some concept of what their ancestral culture may have been, but they do not really know much about their beliefs or traditions. The countries in Europe that currently hold fast to their traditions are frequently looked down upon by Americans as simple or uneducated. This was intentional. Without having reinforced the denial of ancestral traditions, unification of the American population could not be met. This can also be found in the numerous African Americans who do not know which African nation or tribe their own ancestors have come from. Therefore, you will see African American people do things that align with the same goals and objectives as the White population. In this manner, education has been effective. The goal was to reinforce a similar aspirational focus point in all students. To give them the same traditions to celebrate with and to unify the nation with a common religious focus, Christianity.

It is also easy to see the way in which Americans behave fearfully and aggressively toward immigrants who remain steadfast in their cultural heritage while living in America. The immigrants are mocked for their clothing, for their language, for their holidays, and for eating different foods. This is a clear example of narcissistic injury in the citizens who feel they have to reinforce one belief system since their own was taken from them in previous generations.

Additionally, immigrants tend to be business owners. They do not typically come to America seeking jobs. Some do, but many have family owned businesses that they run as a group. This is how they were also supporting their families in their homeland. This is quite common in many non-Western nations. Western nations tend to have education systems that promote the creation of employees, not the creation of business owners.

This is interesting when looking at Asian cultures. They had compulsory education first. They also have family owned businesses. There is a balance in these nations that seems to encourage both finding work through increased education and family owned business. Perhaps the ideal of having an employer is the belief that earnings will be higher. This certainly can be true but isn't always the case. They do seem to be highly competitive to the extent that their suicide rates are the highest among school children worldwide (World Health Organization, 2019). The World Health Organization (2019) states that "suicide is the second leading cause of death among 15-29-year-olds in 2016." The highest suicide rate in the same age group in America is found with the American Indian/Alaskan Native women (American Psychological Association, 2012).

Learning as Science

John Dewey is heralded by educators across the nation as someone who promoted healthy learning. Although this is true, much of his work has been ignored by the modern schooling system. In his book, "How We Think" (1910), Dewey explained childhood learning as a modern representation of scientific thought. His description of this process consisted of five steps.

- A felt difficulty
- Its location and definition
- Suggestions for possible solution
- Development by reasoning of the bearings of the suggestion
- Further observation and experiment leading to its acceptance or rejection; that is, the conclusion of belief or disbelief.

This is now known as the modern scientific method. Dewey's intention was not for this to be exclusive to scientific inquiry. He was describing how people think, which includes children. Alison Gopnik (1996) wrote The Scientist as Child stating, "that scientists are big children." Dewey saw the classroom as a laboratory. This method can be seen in popular Montessori education, which has been around since 1912. Dewey also pointed out that the teachers were also experimenting with the students in their classrooms in order to test new ideas and material (Dewey, 1897). As such, students and teachers were collaborative in classroom experimentation. Dewey found that when children and teachers were given free rein to foster spontaneity, it gave the students the opportunity to create novel solutions (Dewey, 1915). Psychologists in the late 1800's included Darwin's work on evolution in their understanding of how spontaneous ideas were critical to mental development. "Child study" found that when experimenting with children, the children were not filled with self-conscious hesitations the way that adults were. Their ability to communicate and banter ideas helps them to learn and explore ideas. He found thinking to be very social in nature. Schools should be a community of co-investigators since all learning is inclusive of the society in which the application is immediate.

Guides

The predominant aspects found in the previously mentioned methods are highly focused on respecting the child. To that end, if a child is respected, they also learn how to respect. When children can respect their own interests, curiosity, autonomy, and physical body, they develop healthy boundaries and know how to respect healthy boundaries in others. They learn to collaborate, work out solutions respectfully, and inquire without feeling shame. This is the opposite of the dominance model found in most school settings and family homes. This also teaches the students to respond to what is asked of them instead of reacting.

There are numerous schools around the world that offer this type of educational format. They are categorized as democratic schools.

Democratic in that the students have equal voice in their educational experience and the management of their educational society. More independent minded families will choose to do what is known as unschooling. Unschooling does not exclude the attendance of school. Unschooling respects the child's interests and the parent guides the child through support of their interests. They do not teach utilizing curriculum unless the child is interested in learning that way. Instead, they provide resources and opportunities for the child to explore their interest the way that pulls out their highest scientific inquiry capacity. Then there are some families who take this to a global level. These families are utilizing unschooling (with or without curriculum), but also exposing their children to different countries and cultures to expand their child's learning and comprehension of the world in which they live. Worldschooling is also like the way in which nomadic tribes explored and survived. It is as natural as the migration of birds and very strongly rooted in human behavior throughout history.

Another subset focuses on peaceful parenting. This is a method of parenting that does not utilize punishment, but nurtures parent and child relationships. Adults learn to utilize appropriate responses that correlate with the child's current developmental abilities. This relationship is built on a strong foundation of love, trust, and respect. Parents model empathy and cooperate with their children in finding solutions that work for the entire family's needs. Adults have no more say than the children. Everyone's needs are met, and no one feels controlled, ignored, or disempowered. Strategies that peaceful parents utilize look like the following:

- Listening instead of assuming
- Guiding instead of controlling

- Connecting instead of punishing
- Encouraging instead of demanding or ordering
- Responding instead of reacting
- Parent and child discover solutions to problems together instead of children being punished for problems.
- Children learn from their mistakes rather than being punished for them.

Children raised in such an environment develop resiliency and become healthy adults who can respect themselves and others equally. Parents who have opted for this method also find that they heal their own childhood wounds and heal from trauma experienced early on in life. The goal is to build relationships that foster the following traits:

- Compassion
- Emotional regulation
- Intrinsic motivation
- Critical thinking skills
- Conflict resolution skills
- Resiliency
- Responsibility
- Respect of self and others

Families that participate in these types of relationships find that their families are literally more peaceful, cooperative, and do not suffer the complaints most traditional parenting families have. The same can be said for the democratic schools. Their use of respect for all members of the community prevents much of the issues traditional schools suffer from.

~ 15 ~

COMMUNICATION SKILLS

Communication is important in any relationship. Without communication, assumptions and misunderstandings prevail. This creates emotional reactions and behaviors that are counter to effective relationship building or to accomplishing goals. Much of the communication commonly seen in schools and families are more in alignment with maintaining order than they are respecting the individuals in the room. It is as if the individuals are less important than the goal. This is not to be confused with collectivist cultures who are looking for the common good of all involved. This is different. This is meeting the desire of an external party for the good of that party. The family and school are then subservient to the external party's expectations. So, meaningful communication takes a back seat to ensure that the external party is appeased.

Teachers

Who is the external party? Well, in schools, it would be the school district, and the government entities that fund the schools. It is not about the teachers in the classroom and it is not about the students.

Teachers are pressured to perform and to ensure that the students perform up to par. Without this, the teacher may lose their job, or the school may lose their funding. This changes the way in which the teacher communicates with students. Many teachers that I have spoken with became quite defensive when the suggestion of offering children more say in their learning experience was addressed. Every single one of them said that they do not have that kind of time. Although this is what I did in my own classrooms and they saw the results and were pleased, they did not deem it possible to do so in their own classrooms. There are many factors relating to this response.

Many teachers follow set patterns. They adhere to them because this is what they are familiar with and what has worked for them in the past. This does not always mean that it has worked for their students. Spend time in the teachers' lounge and listen to the way they speak of the students who do not adhere to the way they do things in their classroom. They deem these students as the problem. Never once will a teacher take responsibility for their contribution to the situation. Teachers do not have time to deal with individual student needs, so most of these students are removed from the classroom, addressed through special programs, or repeatedly punished in manners that exacerbate their behavior.

Most teachers resort to reward and punishment cycles as previously discussed. The teachers adhere to a hierarchical structure to maintain their classrooms, which does not bode well for teaching students about democracy or how to behave in a democracy. For students living in a nation founded on the principles of democracy, this is very problematic. There is only one place that a student can experience democracy and that is through their student governance clubs, but not in their daily lives. One could easily argue that students were being trained to work in hierarchical employment scenarios. These employment scenarios are also lacking in democratic structure and are often rife with abuses. Any number of discrimination cases that have gone before the courts were in direct relationship to the non-democratic fashion in which our schools and places of employment operate. To have an equal and just society, then democracy must be exercised daily in everyday environments so that true accountability and responsibility can be developed fully.

Families

Who is the external party for families? Families answer to more than one. They answer to the school and they answer to the employers of the adult family members. They currently have the least say in their experience, even within their own homes.

Schools pressure parents to continue the school's job at home. This is to reinforce learning and ensure that the child has ample opportunity to reinforce learning that was sanctioned by the school district. Parents also must adhere to their own work demands. This can inhibit their schedules, their mental focus, and their stress levels with their own families. Having their livelihood threatened can have a grave impact on family communication and healthy relationship development.

What do children learn from this? Parents are often so focused on providing for their children and being there for their children's numerous activities, that they don't even realize the way in which they communicate with their children frequently disempowers them and sets them up for greater failures as adults. This in turn, sets the child up to have a more difficult time with their own employment scenarios and feeling inadequate as a parent. Many parents shower their children with material items that they felt were denied to them when they were children. Without realizing what their actions do, they teach their children that they are deserving of anything regardless of their own contribution to the environment.

Parents disempower their children by telling them that the failures they experience are not their fault. Parents may blame the coach or the teacher for the child's failure to make the child feel more confident. This only teaches the child to believe they are above reproach and they are never adequately challenged to improve their efforts so that they can feel truly proud of their accomplishments. This encourages the victimhood narcissistic behavior patterns that will also flourish in adulthood and ruin future employment and family relationships. Children do not learn responsibility and accountability with this method of communication.

Focus

What should be focused on is what is within the child's control. In order to raise resilient children who take responsibility and accountability for their actions, parents and teachers need to encourage the child's autonomy. Knowing that the child is responsible for the outcome and that someone else can't take it away from them or decide for them how it will turn out, empowers a child to focus intently on their goal and what they must do to achieve it. They are responsible entirely for the results because they were autonomous in their efforts. They can have a guide by the side to assist them in their effort, but to have the entire instructions and order of business dictated to from an external source makes the child remove the focus from their own effort and instead makes them focus on pleasing. Pleasing is a behavior that is found in the fawning trauma response. This conditions children to be eager to please any outside source that puts their value above the child's value. It puts the responsibility on the external source who can later be blamed when it does not go as desired. The hopeless belief of victimhood becomes far too easily obtained. These fall within the narcissistic abuse spectrum of behavior patterns.

It is far more important to show children that they are not powerless or at the behest of others who are bigger and stronger than they are. They should rely upon adults to protect them from harm, but not to be an additional source of harm regardless of how normalized the behavior is in society. What this creates are adults who know that they can change their outcomes because they know they are the sole responsible party for their life. This is stated in many places, but not held in practice as most adults feel they are dependent upon an employer or other external source for their basic survival. We do not have an empowered society that feels capable of taking their own lives completely into their own hands. Very few feel they can start their own businesses, yet prior to the industrial revolution, most families owned their own businesses. In fact, it is quite normal in most countries around the world for families to own their own businesses and not seek external employment sources. It is critical that we do not undermine children's confidence and problem-solving skills through robbing them of autonomy.

Disempowered children become disempowered adults who will chronically see that there is no way forward and that they are permanently held at the behest of forces greater than themselves. This makes them give up and give excuses rather than find solutions to their problems. This is an avoidance behavior that can also be identified in the trauma responses. Many who fall into this area tend to have chronic behaviors such as lying and manipulating others to get what they want. They do not believe that being stronger as autonomous individuals will succeed because they have never experienced it. They only know what they were raised and taught with.

Disempowered adults create disempowered children, thus creating more disempowered adults.

Children mirror the behaviors of the adults they are exposed to. If the teachers and parents are disempowered and under an external control, the children will learn to hold themselves down in order to maintain what is familiar to them. Much of this has to do with the way in which adults communicate with them.

Communicate

There are numerous ways in which adults communicate with children. Very seldom are adults communicating in an empowering way with children. Much of what we see between adults and children is dominance oriented. Adults talk down to children to demand obedience or to establish power. Other adults praise everything the child does regardless of the activity or choices made by the child. Neither of these options provide a healthy reflection for the child to learn from. Children do not learn autonomy under either option. One instills fear while the other instills contempt. Fear is a major factor in abuse and the results have been discussed in previous chapters. The contempt aspect is a direct result of the child not having a strong platform from which they can interpret what is safe and good for them. No guidance was offered when it was requested. Children are intelligent, and they always ask for what they need. Many adults do not listen.

Adults should never talk at a child. Adults need to engage with a child in mutual conversation for the child's mind to develop healthy connections in the brain that can help them navigate the world more effectively. This requires a conversation of equals. Without equality, the child's brain will automatically go into survival responses, and those development patterns become learned behaviors for the rest of their lives. To program children through survival that is not a legitimate threat, is to program the mind to respond maladaptively to real world experiences. This has long-term consequences on their ability to function in society and within their interpersonal relationships. Communicating as equals also provides the child language processing skills that they can use throughout their lifetime, which will empower their autonomous success far into adulthood. Ways in which communication can be accomplished look like the following examples:

- Listen to children. Do not talk at them or direct them.
- Mirror safety and order - do not be the chaos or something to fear.
- Allow children to freely play and explore independently.
- Allow children space and opportunities to fail and struggle.
- Make your communication an intentional effort to understand.

Boundaries are developed in children by exposure to boundaries in adults. If the adult feels entitled to violate another's boundaries, the child will violate another's boundaries. This includes adults violating children's boundaries. This can be emotional, physical, or intellectual.

Provide guidance by the side. Help the child understand what they are exploring when they ask. Do not decide for them what they are to learn. Let them determine what they wish to learn and then provide the materials they need to do this and help them when they request it. Do not interrupt them. Express your boundaries and limits in a respectful manner. This teaches children to also express their boundaries and limits in a respectful manner. Then respect those boundaries and limits.

Frequent areas that are commonly used by adults toward children that are counter to the above examples include speaking to children in impatient and demanding ways. Doing so teaches the children to also respond in impatient and demanding ways. The following examples are common communication skills used by adults with children that do not adhere to patience and respect of the child (or anyone else they are speaking to in this manner):

- What's wrong with you?
- Be patient!
- You're fine. Stop crying.
- Calm down
- Stop making a big deal about it
- It's not scary. Come on do it anyway. You'll be fine.
- Eat all of your food.
- Be quiet
- Sit still
- Stop complaining/whining
- Because I said so
- Don't be silly
- Don't talk back
- Come on give your aunt a hug or grandma a kiss
- You can't have it until you say please
- I will take "something important" away from you if you don't do what I say.

After reviewing this list, it is likely that the reader will find themselves feeling stress after identifying behavior patterns that they may have. This may also be followed by defending these choices and cognitive dissonance may start to take over. However, after deep re-flection, it should be obvious how these word choices are domineer-ing and disempowering to anyone who should be on the receiving end of them. These are condescending and disrespectful words. They do not represent safety or consideration of the child's feelings or needs. It is all about the adult. What this teaches the child is how to disempower others and that they are of little value. I do not believe that this is the goal that any adult would want in guiding children as they grow into maturity.

The goal is to raise responsible adults who will take care of their lives and families, yet we raise and teach children to be afraid of not pleasing the adults in their lives who become angry with the child for not letting the adult control them. Responsibility does not grow out of being controlled. What comes from being controlled in trained trauma behavior. This disengages the victim's mind from the pur-pose behind the action other than to avoid future injury from the person(s) who is the most current threat to their survival. Manipu-lation and external influence do not create responsible and account-able adults. Instead, the dominating person takes responsibility away from them, creating disempowered people. Simultaneously, the per-son taking the responsibility away blames the other person for not meeting their demands as they see fit, which is ultimately what nar-cissistic abusers do. This is an abuse cycle.

Relationships and Self-Control

Jacobs (1998) wrote that, "Self-discipline develops not by being si-lenced, punished, or inhibited, but by being permitted to express and act on the longings that represent the child's deepest nature" (p.188). Children who are listened to and consciously paid attention to develop healthy relationships with the adults in their environment. This nurtures the child's autonomous development and reinforces mutual respect between child and caregiver or educator. Children are inquisitive by nature. They do not need encouragement to learn. Without intervention, they will learn far more by following their natural curiosity than any school system's mandates could require of them. The freedom to explore and investigate provides natural learning and consequence comprehension development. This instills a deeper sense of sincerity and earnest in endeavors pursued. "When the central purpose in life is empowering others, Authority over them becomes hypocritical" (Jacobs, 1998, p. 181). So how can this be accomplished in our schools and homes?

How Democratize A Classroom

We can begin by democratizing our classrooms. What does that look like and what can be expected? Since most adults have never experienced this type of treatment in their own childhoods, they will be skeptical and fearful of how to manage such an attempt. It may be challenging at first as the teacher explores their own programmed abuse and behavior patterns. Do not be offended that you do harbor such tendencies. Any adult who was raised in a hierarchical environment has them. That is what they were taught. As such, this requires a lot of self-control by the adult as they explore their own programmed behaviors and watch those in correlation to the responses given by the children. The children are also in homes that utilize this type of structure as most parents were raised the same way. That may make this sound impossible to achieve, but it is not. I have done this in numerous schools within hierarchical school systems and with parents who had no idea what democracy in a classroom. Many did not know how to speak respectfully to children. Children learn very quickly. The biggest obstacle lies in the way the children will not trust the teacher. This is in direct correlation with their survival instincts from previous ill treatment. As such, they are not going to readily believe that the adult trusts and respects them. That will be the first sign that there is programmed trauma in the children already.

Trust is a huge component of this. This means that the children must be trusted. This means teachers need firm boundaries that students cannot violate. Students cannot violate each other or themselves, and the teacher cannot violate the students. This involves helping them to nominate their own classroom governance. There is no room for fear as fear is the essence of chaos. Whatever transpires, the teacher implementing this newly formed government cannot be deterred when the most traumatized children test to see if the teacher is sincere in trusting and respecting them. They all come around. The children with the least trauma adapt immediately. It is so smooth; the teacher will wonder why they never did it before. For those addressing children in extreme trauma background environments, it may take a lot longer. It is important that the teacher adhere to this no matter how difficult it may seem at times. It always does work and once it does, the remainder of the school year is so smooth that you will accomplish far more than if you had remained strict with hierarchical authority structure. Most importantly, the children develop a healthy relationship with the teacher, and this fosters a much greater learning environment for the students and the teacher collectively. If the teacher remains steadfast results are guaranteed.

I would highly recommend making this shift at the beginning of the school year because the students are new to the teacher and have no preconceived expectations of how the classroom is run. However,

I have personally done this in the middle of the year, and it went very smoothly. I have done this in 7 different schools and the ages ranged between 4th grade - middle school. There are numerous schools who operate completely democratically, and they have students ranging from pre-K - 12th grade. Age is not an issue in this application. What is an issue, is the teacher's ability to fully implement and be comfortable with application.

The struggle will remain with the teacher, not the students. They will be highly interested in what is being done. They will find it vastly different than what they have experienced in any other school. Most will be excited that they have control and as such, they take this role very seriously and vehemently uphold the rules and regulations established by their collective decisions.

The few students that may question this process are the students that typically found themselves in trouble utilizing the more traditional classroom management procedures. They have been burnt before and are very mistrustful of anything that looks like they will be given any control. The message they have been told in the past is that they aren't trustworthy. When suddenly given control, the following responses may occur:

- They will test the rules to see if the teacher was serious.
- They will make a mockery out of it to see if other students will agree with them.
- They will try to find a way to create a resistance between themselves and the teacher or even perhaps themselves and the students (but their main focus will always be the teacher because historically that's where the true resistance usually took place).

What becomes apparent as the process moves on, is that the resistors will suddenly become the heaviest enforcers and they will simultaneously and eagerly take their own punishments because they had some ownership in creating them. What will happen is that the teacher no longer must issue threats of any kind. The teacher's role will simply be to teach! This process also works well in flipped classrooms. In fact, I personally feel that a flipped democratic classroom is the ideal situation for public schools. Sometimes that is not entirely possible due to subject matter or logistics.

The only issues I have found with this type of process were not really a problem with the process as much as the location in which I was expected to teach. If the teaching space is highly inappropriate for effective learning, the democratic process will not be any easier to implement. It can be done, but it may take a little longer to be fully effective and will likely require dividing students up into smaller groups with more autonomy.

When in difficult learning environments, the teacher needs to give more control over to the students, dividing them up into smaller groups with leaders in each group who are then given the ability to make decisions for their group. It is highly effective to allow students to teach others. The most difficult students are frequently effective group leaders. The difficult students are often quite intelligent and are thrilled that they are given the opportunity to take on a meaningful role and be involved in their class in a way they normally never experience.

This is the protocol that I have utilized. Teachers can experiment with variations of this which work for them and the situations they find themselves in:

1. I introduce myself to the students and explain to them that things will work differently in your classroom from what they are used to experiencing.

2. I explain to the students that they will nominate rules for the class and that after the nominations of rules, we will take a vote on those rules and use the rules most heavily voted for as our classroom rules. (Clearly anything that jeopardizes the safety of anyone is not an option and please be sure to clarify to the students anything that makes that option invalid. Ensure that it is not an opinion, but a true hazard or something which can harm others. Give the students full autonomy to make meaningful decisions for themselves and the safety of their group. They will genuinely surprise with their insights).

Most of the classrooms voted on keeping approximately 4-5 of the nominated rules. Democratically run schools often have more rules than traditional schools because the students become very aware of what they want and do not want to experience in their learning environment. Teachers should not limit students if they feel they need more rules that are important to them. Honor the students' beliefs. Teacher's thoughts are equally valuable and shared with the class for the group to consider. It is important to do so in a way that is honest and not manipulative. The teacher should ask them questions about their choices that make them consider the implications of their decisions.

3. Once the rules have been voted on, students will then have to nominate consequences for violating those rules. Typically, I have them vote on a set pattern of "consequences" that they can apply to all rules. If you have unusual pairing of rules and consequences, then clearly individualized consequences can be implemented. I focus on keeping things as clear, simple, and straightforward as possible so that no one can be confused by the implementation. After nominations of consequences have been done, take a vote on each one.

4. The teacher or selected student then writes the nominations on the board, if one is available, or takes notes so that the nominations can easily be repeated back to the group. The teacher should also clarify for the students what the meaning of their own nominated expectations are so that everyone clearly understands what they're voting on. Think of this as a Presidential election. Their lives are involved, and the future of their community will be seriously impacted by these decisions. Take this very seriously.

5. Insert a process of monitors for the classroom rules. Change "guard" weekly or daily as the teacher and students see fit. No student should be left out of this role. Every student has a right to make the rules, and every student has a right to enforce them. Make the voted rules and consequences visible so that regardless of who is in charge that day/week will not

forget the processes voted on or the next step in the consequences if they have to handle something.

When the students are self-monitoring, they will be much more participatory in the daily activities, and the students who caused trouble in the past will suddenly come alive and be much more involved in learning and in behavior management of themselves and others.

How to Democratize A School

The same concerns mentioned in democratizing a classroom still apply to the school setting. However, the transition may be easier to adjust the school structure if done methodically from younger grades and then grow with those students as they move upward in the grades.

Individual teachers will run their classrooms democratically for the full engulfment of school democracy to be effective and realized. Once all teachers are functioning in this platform, the hierarchical structure of school governance is then in place. Each classroom will have nominated their "Senators" or "Congressmen" (mere name suggestions) and those representatives will then be part of the larger school meeting where larger school functioning decisions can be made.

Weekly meetings should be encouraged, and representatives of the staff should also be elected. The realization that the adults are just as responsible to the children's expectations as the children are to the adults' expectations must be tightly acknowledged and adhered to. If the children feel that they are part of some sham government, it will completely disintegrate and waste everyone's time. If they feel that their decisions have real impact (like voting in America- many don't vote because they feel they will have no impact), they will be fully engaged and take their roles very seriously. They will participate in making school-wide decisions that impact rules/regulations/social decisions for all students and teachers/staff. Adult votes are equally significant as student votes in the meetings. True equality equals true democracy.

Where else can students learn what democracy is if they never experience it in their formative years? There can be guidelines that are non-negotiable, such as safety and district-wide regulations/state regulations. Clearly there are parameters that cannot be changed. However, if adults find issues with any suggestion mentioned or considered by the student representatives, they are just as welcome to share their thoughts and concerns with the group before any voting or decision making is passed. A breakdown of how this would be structured is as follows:

1. Each classroom votes for their class representative. This can be done weekly, monthly, semester/quarterly or annually. A change of representative should be honored frequently so that all the students have a deeper understanding of what that level of responsibility is like and how much impact it has on others.

2. Each representative meets in a weekly meeting with representatives from the staff (who ideally were also voted on by other staff).

3. Meetings include an agenda (just like board meetings) where issues are brought to the table, discussed, solutions offered, and then solutions are voted upon. Once voted upon, they become the guideline upon which the school must operate

until otherwise changed by another meeting or larger entity (district/state) overrides the decision. Motion carries - just like all other adult meetings we experience in America. Treat the children as leaders and respect their feelings and thoughts. Adults share thoughts as equally as students share theirs. Adults and students bring up concerns for consideration. Adults cannot belittle student choices. Instead, adults should offer solutions effectively explaining why and how they impact everyone. Give students the opportunity to consider what kind of impact their choices will have, without making them feel inferior or insignificant.

4. Make an announcement to the entire school that informs the teachers, staff, and other students what the student/staff governance has decided so that the implementation can be made effective upon a specified date. Be very communicative. No one can make informed decisions without authentic communication. The students are more inclined to adhere to the guidelines as they have personally selected the representative, they informed their representative of the issue they wanted brought to the council and they see action made upon that concern.

To make such a major transition in a larger public school, a gradual process may need to be implemented. Perhaps in a high school, it could be implemented immediately, but democratic schools who have experience with transitioning students out of traditional school models to democratic models have found the effectiveness of implementing full democracy in a school is more difficult for children who were treated differently prior to 12 years of age. There will be more struggles in the initial implementation because the students will not trust or believe that they were given control. However, it is possible.

It relies more upon the steadfastness of the staff in ensuring effective implementation. It will require a lot of effort, patience, and self-control on the part of the adults involved.

The best strategy is to begin this with the kindergarten grade. Run a small democracy between their classrooms only. Then as they grow up in grades, implement it in the next grade level, and so on and so forth as they become older. After 6 years, your entire elementary school will be fully democratized. You can do the same with the middle schools and high schools. However, if done with the initial class that began from kindergarten, they will already know how to function and will be much more effective at helping the teachers and staff adapt to the process rather than the staff having to struggle with their own lack of experience and knowledge about such a philosophy.

It will be longer than a decade, but 10 years is a small price to pay for a lifetime of smooth-running schools that teach young people

- how to live in a democracy,
- who then understand the value of their vote as adults,
- who are autonomous and know how they affect others,
- and who feel heard and represented.

Many of the struggles currently found in our schools will be solved by changing how we view children and their ability to self-govern.

Resources are available at the Alternative Education Resource Organization for further reading and support on how to implement and understand educational structure from this standpoint. There are over a century's worth of well-researched and applied insights available, which will positively impact how our schools operate with the involvement of student governance. These resources can be found at http://educationrevolution.org.

How to Democratize at Home

As mentioned in the previous sections, this requires more effort on behalf of the adults to unprogram themselves than it does for the children. Children who will struggle are those who have had no voice in their experiences prior. They will not feel safe knowing that they are suddenly in a new environment that trusts them, and they may challenge this to see if it is true. If the home was already respectful, it will be a smooth transition and no major issues should occur. The health of the family will be obvious in the implementation based upon the reactions of those who feel insecure or threatened in their position as authority or rebellion against authority. Once the whole family operates democratically, removal of the resistance and much of what common parenting conversations contain disappears. Rebellious children do not occur in respectful home environments. They result from being disrespected and controlled.

To keep this as simple as possible, it is most important to focus on the way in which everyone in the house communicates with one another. Disrespectful word choices and tones are not allowed as they do not offer a healthy platform for anyone to feel heard and respected. That means apologies are required and everyone is given the opportunity to correct their choices and try again. This will be especially critical in the beginning. It is important to discuss behaviors that are bothersome, but not in a way that calls another any kind of derogatory name. Talk about behavior, not identity.

If a simple family rule should be made, the most effective is that anyone can do anything they want in the house if they are not violating anyone else's experience. It sounds simplistic, yet it truly covers every single issue that anyone could possibly have with any other family member. It also reinforces autonomy and natural consequences. If a child chooses something that does not violate anyone else, but ultimately violates themselves in some manner, they will naturally experience the consequences of that choice. An example might include not going to bed and accomplishing sufficient sleep.

If any family member has been violated, then they are entitled to discuss the issue with the party who did the violation. Again, this should be discussed as a behavior and not an identity label. Name calling is not constructive. Telling a sibling that their choice to stay up all night impacted others in the house is appropriate. They need to understand how they impact others as much as they learn how they impact themselves. If there are repetitive issues, then the family should have a meeting to discuss boundaries, rules, and consequences to address the issue. The person who committed the offense is equally heard and has an equal vote. It is important that they are involved so that they have equal power in their own experience. Ultimately, the family members will learn to not violate one another nor to violate themselves. This is a critical skill for boundary development that can also be implemented in the larger social community. This will prevent potential abuse from outsiders as well. Children who learn that they have a right to not be violated, will not allow others to violate them.

~ 16 ~

PRACTICAL APPLICATION

After thorough examination of the history of education in the United States, the psychological conditioning tactics utilized and the source of these strategies, it is crucial to consider the impact that these efforts have had on our society. We have had well over a century of compulsory education with these strategies in place, so it is now that we can state there is sufficient evidence to the outcomes provided by these efforts. The rise in behaviors issues, violence, and decline in academic achievement should be the most obvious visual demonstrations of how we have failed our society and our youth. Now that there is increasing research in epigenetics and neuroscience, there is further evidence that the efforts done have had long-term and generational impact on collective groups of society. The inclusion of psychiatric medication started in the 1990's and has continued to increase and be utilized with younger and younger children before their brains have developed. Most evident is the lack of adult self-reflection to question their own contribution to the problem. The blame was always placed on the children.

Historic Success Despite Education

There have been numerous examples of adults who succeeded in exemplary fashion despite their educational outcomes and lack of degree completion. This is also often overlooked, and students are never encouraged to explore their world through their own motivations, but rather the prescribed plan provided by the adults in their lives. Students who demonstrate independent interests and what is deemed "defiant" behavior toward forced conforming to classroom norms are often highly intelligent. They are frequently denied an appropriate platform from which they can develop their own skills. Others have achieved the highest offices in the nation despite their inferior educational scores. Education and its testing mechanisms demonstrate little example of a student's capacity for success in life. Some of this is privilege due to race, sex, or class. Others are more independently focused despite their education and refuse to be deterred from their personal goals. These are often students who were not encouraged in any particular area but were often constantly redirected to other things that parents and teachers felt the child should focus on. Many adults have a habit of ignoring their children's natural instincts and talents and frequently fear that their child will not succeed if they are not doing what the other children are doing. Some feel pressure for their children to succeed so that they can be approved of by their community and peers. Again, this is about the adults, not the children.

Purpose of Education for Life

The most important aspect of what education really means for life is not for the benefit of the children. Education is the primary source of childcare for millions of Americans who need to work outside of the home. Since schools are covered by taxation, families feel that they can benefit from the seemingly free childcare and their children will simultaneously learn something to make them more successful in their future adult lives. This is the extent of the interest that parents have with schools. Some may be into the competitions and eager to prove that their child is the best. This is again about the adult, not about the child. Children are being used for adult needs.

Even further, the education industry in America is the largest employer. There are many different sub-employers varying from school district staff to curriculum publishers, desk creators, school cafeteria supplies and the agriculture department. In recent decades, this has also begun to include the medical industry, the psychiatric and pharmaceutical industries, the prison industry, and the police industry. Manufacture of technology and materials for students to use is an even broader brush of how much the education machine supports the American economy. The children are being used for adult needs.

Danger in Education

The dangers involved in the education system have been increasing at greater and greater rates in recent decades. The increase of police on campus, guns on campus, school shootings, campuses being locked down during school hours, and the increased surveillance on students in their school as well as through technology used for school at home is preparing these children for a life of living in a police state. They will not question its presence since it was normalized to them during their most formative years.

The increased drugging of children is also feeding the increased use of recreational drug use by youth, which not only contributes to damage in their developing brains, but it increases their potential for finding themselves inside of the criminal justice system at some point. Some find themselves targeted for behavior more vehemently than other students due to race or class. The education system has consistently reinforced discrimination despite policies that state otherwise for employees.

Subject Focus

What many teachers of the arts and similar subjects that are frequently left out of the standardized testing machine feel is that they are treated as if what they do is entertain the children. Many teachers look at the arts and physical education teachers as welcome distractions to their busy day teaching academics. Some students need physical education and arts education to cope with their individual trauma experiences. Some are gifted and talented in these areas. What numerous research studies have pointed out over the last 30 years is how critical these subjects are to brain development, physical development, motor skills, and brain body connectivity. The arts are especially critical to creating more interconnectivity between brain hemispheres, thus making intellectual capacity more advanced and efficient. Yet these subjects are treated by school districts as disposable fluff topics. School administrators and board members rarely read research studies on these subjects and how they impact brain development and overall physical health development for minds and bodies that are literally developing during their watch every single day. This is negligence.

Cultural Impact

"That's real power. When you can eliminate or paralyze identity, make your enemies' cultures either nonexistent or criminal then you've done one better than genocide—you've made it so that not only is your enemy gone, she never even existed." (Mosley, 2018).

One area that numerous researchers have been trying to address is the dismissal of cultural identity in the classroom. Many schools have been tasked with stripping individual cultures of their cultural traditions and identity to generate a uniform "American" identity and culture. Although this may have possibly had a theoretical good intention at the inception of this process over one hundred years ago, the results that we see today tell another story. Cultures who are more solidified in holding on to their identity find themselves facing discrimination and racism in America every single day. Even the cultures who have tried to assimilate still find this true. The stripping of culture does not remove the deeper need that people have of their own cultural identity. This is a wound that has been pushed for too long and needs full rectification. This includes individual tribal culture identities for all American citizens from every single continent. Of course, there really is not "time" for this in the daily curriculum to accomplish the limited testing sanctions. The current focus is clearly doing more harm than it is good.

Democratic Schools

Democracy requires participation from the whole society, not just certain groups. Democracy also requires equal representation of all viewpoints before the whole group votes on the rule of order that should govern the society. This includes consequences being discussed and voted on by all citizens.

This is how democratic schools operate. They are actual democracies. If adults were put above children, then it is not a democracy, it is an authoritarian hierarchy. America is also an authoritarian hierarchy. Manipulation is done to appease people just enough to make them feel like they were heard, but their voices were never included in the decision nor did they truly have access to the bills in order to vote on them. The bills are also written in such convoluted ways and they may talk of one major topic, but there are other topics sandwiched in to inadvertently pass additional laws without citizens being aware. They make it appear to be too difficult for regular citizens to participate in and teach the citizens to elect someone they think is smarter who represents their feelings. They are later disappointed when that smarter person listens, but still votes the way they see fit.

It is problematic having votes from those who are ignorant of the whole picture. If we were educated, this would never be an issue, but we are not educating our society. The "education" is primarily focused on behavioral conditioning and exposure to things, but no real meaningful purpose is met by the end of the many years spent in school. Job skills are not obtained. The only reason there would need to be a behavioral conditioning program is to teach people how to follow authority. They are not learning democracy.

Another common aspect found in the various types of democratic schools in operation around the world, is that they allow the students to choose their interests. There are teachers, schools, and facilities. There is food service and need for transportation. What is not needed is rigid curriculum and testing protocols. Can they test? Sure. The students and teachers discuss what they want to learn and teachers with those areas of expertise form classes for them to teach the students this subject or focus area. Whatever the students sign up for, they are required to complete. So, students have full control over their experience and they also own full responsibility for their learning. If they choose to not take any class, that is allowed as well. They can study independently in the school whatever topic that interests them. They can do this through various methods and for as long as they wish.

Students who first attend democratic schools, after having been in a traditionally structured school environment, do often go through a deschooling phase. They do not believe that the adults are serious about allowing them to choose their schedule and learning experience. This is like the behavior discussed in the communication chapter. Deschooling is really untraumatizing. They are recovering from programmed behavior designed to make them respond in one of the four trauma responses (fight, flight, freeze, or fawn). Sometimes this can take a little while. The student can spend their time on campus however they wish, but they are not allowed to disturb the learning process of the other students.

The governance of the school includes all students and teachers, so the behavior that falls outside of the voted-on rules are addressed by the school governance at the next meeting. When a new student experiences this and feels that they have ownership over their entire experience, including their own violation of school rules, they tend to start taking the process more seriously as they have witnessed how it works. I would say that those with deeper trauma history may take longer to adjust.

What these schools foster is social justice. They foster responsibility. They foster accountability. They foster equality and respect for others. There is no hierarchy or competition designed to harm others and put anyone in a position of dominance over another. If we wish to fix our nation so that the entire population knows how to behave in an ethical, socially just, and respectful manner, we have to abolish the current focus of our educational system toward one that actually empowers learning and teaches students how these pieces work together toward a more constructive outcome that all benefit from.

Unschooling

Unschooling is a form of homeschooling that follows a similar path as the democratic school process. Unschooling can vary dramatically from family to family. In this instance, the entire family has to go through the deschooling process and un-traumatize themselves from the norms that they had been conditioned to previously. It also teaches them how to have healthier family relationships that empower the entire family to work in conjunction with each other's goals and no one person takes full responsibility of everyone else's needs. Democratic schools have mixed ages, so there are older students helping younger students throughout the day. The same is true in an unschooling family. There is no division of grade in either scenario, so children can learn from anyone in the home and anyone in their community as they go about their day. Parents are only tasked to be the guide by the side and to pay attention to the interests of their children so that they can foster the learning process that is occurring. This does not mean never-ending field trips or numerous planned activities. Additionally, children can play a significant contributing role in planning activities and any outings taken by the family so that they are also learning planning, navigation, logistics, and considering the needs of the group. Taking ownership of the experience teaches them far more than students who are taken on a forced trip that was pre-determined for them and they are only required to attend, behave, and participate as required.

Unschooling does not mean a "power shift" from parents to kids, regarding their learning. The power to learn or not learn is always ultimately in the hands of the learner, no matter what kind of schooling is done. This is such a major mind-shift for those who have no concept of unschooling. Literally every adult I have spoken to outside of the unschoolers I know, immediately assume that it is Lord of the Flies. The concept that there always needs to be one in domination and one in submission. Democracy does not flourish in this power dynamic. Abuse does. This also truncates psychological and professional development. It truncates relationships in marriage. It sets everyone up for failure. Expectations can never be met when placed on both domination and submission. It is unnatural and rife with psychological trauma.

Don't suck the life out of learning.
Life is learning.
Learning is life.
The two are inseparable.
School is not life.
Life is not school.
Unschool and get back to life.

Unschooling means the adult follows the child's lead. If they want to go to Montessori school, they are still unschooling. If they want to go to public school, they are still unschooling. The difference lies in the intention to honor the child's choice. Now, the child has to participate as they have chosen, so this reinforces making decisions for themselves. Unschooling isn't a free-for-all of irresponsibility. It is honoring the child, providing what they need when they want to focus on something, and ensuring that they understand fully what they pursue.

The only time parents are not "unschooling" is when they are making decisions for the child or allowing others or institutions to make decisions for the child. Truly, the term unschooling is insufficient. It is used as a demonstration of the opposite of school in that it does not use coercive control to induce learning.

Unschooling is so much bigger than choosing to not put children in school and letting them make decisions regarding what they are interested in learning. Unschooling means adults have to change their entire perception of the world. It means they have to change their entire perception of how to behave in relationships. It means they must change their entire perception of how they perceive work and earning money. It means they must change their entire perception of nation and place. That may sound extreme, but freedom requires taking ownership of your life. Ownership means responsibility. Undoing the damage of authoritarianism is extremely hard. It requires significant stamina and unwavering strength to get through it. A peaceful and functioning society is worth it in the end. Contempt is developed and it is in direct correlation to being controlled by outside forces.

Unschooling, as the parent, means healing from childhood wounds. It means discovering identity. It means finding out that normal was abuse. It means finding out that everyone deserves freedom and it empowers people to live in a manner that respects them and others. There is no need to be desperate and there is no need to be tough to survive the abuse of others because boundaries are healthy and strong. There is no constant issue in relationships, success, and survival. It is probably the most empowering thing that a person can choose. Moving in the world is not a struggle, but an exploration.

To truly unschool, parents must learn what actual respect means. They must learn what not violating others to take care of their own life means. They must learn that letting others live as they wish without violating themselves is respect. They can do whatever they want if they are not violating someone else, including themselves. That is not our current society and all it teaches. Our current society is in a control dynamic.

Worldschooling

There are some families who take this learning concept of unschooling and they apply it to global learning. This involves global travel and exposure to the world rather than only reading about it. Some travel faster than others. Some spend years in one country or place. Worldschooling offers a level of learning that is elusive in any educational setting. Immersion is the best teaching method. This involves higher order thinking that school cannot replicate. It also teaches the family how different cultures view the world and how customs impact worldview. There will also be common themes found regardless of destination. These are the truths that will remain consistent for students throughout and as such they will be reinforced and remembered. There is no need for testing when the world is your classroom and life is a nonstop new experience.

As far as the need for familiarity or routine, these are things developed within the family that remain the same no matter the location in which they currently reside. This can include family meals, sleeping routines, and time to work and play. Schedules can be maintained no matter where in the globe a family could find themselves. The consistency is found within the family unit and the normal they have created for themselves. Since children are also involved in the planning, they have a voice and a role in the decision making. This includes planning of trips and outings taken by the family. No one is taken anywhere against their will. Respect of each individual remains, and family bonding becomes more important.

Alternative to Traditional Schools

If attending a democratic school or utilizing the previously mentioned family derived educational options are not realistic for a family or the community, it is possible for traditional schools to evolve. The communications chapter discussed how to convert a public school into a democratic school through the governance. As far as the learning platform, schools can discuss their options and find solutions that work for everyone. One thing to remember is that to ensure a healthy society results from these efforts, respecting the wishes of children cannot be secondary. In order to teach children their responsibility to their community and to their own autonomous development, they have to be involved.

Conclusion

Success is a result of confidence and healthy boundaries. Most of what inhibits our society has much to do with narcissistic abuse strategies that are normalized in our systems and society at large. The further support provided by neuroscience, epigenetics, and psychology reinforce the need to change our current educational trajectory. The society we currently find ourselves in is a direct result of our educational system. Literally every single person, with rare exception, was formed in that system. How is it manifesting? Is it healthy? Is social justice and equality present? Is discrimination and abuse chronic? Are the needs of an economic machine more important than the safety and survival of our children and future society? What kind of future do we want for our society?

Our current systems have trained everyone to participate in a narcissistic abuse system. Reward and punishment, carrot dangling promises, and harsh sanctions for noncompliance are so common that the motivation most people have is for short-term gains and nothing that ensures they consider the larger picture of what they are participating in or subjecting their families to. Obedience over self-respect is quite common. Legal persecution and threat are utilized to reinforce the current strategies within the schools so that teachers do not stray from the behavioral conditioning process. Economic stability and job security take precedence over consideration of what they are doing to the children in their care. Their intentions may be pure, but even teachers feel disrespected and abused. Allegiance to the abusive system trumps self-respect and respecting children. The message received by these developing minds is one of subjugation or dominance. There is no capacity to teach equality and social justice in such a structure. It is counter-intuitive, a complete contradiction.

The separation of school from life sets people up to separate navigating the world and communicating with others in a constructive manner. It turns into a free-for-all dominance competition. Rather than serving as each other's teachers and students, we turn into people who feel we have to prove we're right over literally anyone else and then people feel attacked if they are corrected. The way one is corrected is part of the issue. Most people assert their "knowledge" in a form of dominance over the other, thus the crumbling of any constructive debate or mutual navigation of the topic. The largest factor to really pay attention to is that the dominating behavior is reactionary. It is not responsive.

Reaction is a means for manipulation and directing others to lose their self-control. This makes people easier to control. When they are out of control, they are convinced to buy anything. They react the way the manipulator wants them to. They are emotionally volatile. They often lack self-control. This is done intentionally.

To have a healthy country, we have to start by communicating like the perfect classroom environment where the teacher speaks from a position of understanding and not speaking condescendingly. The teacher may offer another way to see the situation and offer alternatives for consideration. The challenge with this is that it requires people to be patient with one another. It requires time. When I tried to introduce this to public school teachers through means of introducing democracy for classroom management, their #1 response was, "we don't have time for that." This means they prefer a school year of power battles over a one-time effort to establish healthy boundaries and communication.

We live in a time of unprecedented access to information. There is no reason to continue education as it has been. The only threat to this is if governments should start limiting access to information and controlling what people know. This was previously done through curriculum design and there is no reason why they will not implement such strategies on our technology and Internet information access. What this really suggests is that we need to learn how to have an actual democracy. This means that we cannot have a hierarchical dominance structure that tells others what they can and cannot have access to. Individual schools and families should be able to make decisions for themselves on what they want access to.

Are there ill-minded individuals who will attempt to prey upon citizens? Currently, yes. This is what we have created. It will take time to eradicate what we have created. We must start with the children. This requires stamina, determination, and self-control. It also requires self-liberation and deschooling of our adult population so that they can heal their traumas and not perpetuate it on future generations. To bring our human species to a more natural state that functions in ecological respect with its natural surroundings while maintaining the progress we have made; we need to stop the trauma.

What we currently have is a society that does not see anyone else. People only see themselves when they communicate with others. What they see is what aligns with who they are. Anything that does not match that is categorized as a potential threat. This is basic narcissistic categorization and it does not offer higher order thinking capacity. This is an extremely dangerous society in which to live. Hypervigilance is no longer for rare threats of survival; it is a chronic daily state of being. The cost to the psychological development and impact on the health of the human body has been demonstrated in numerous research studies. We literally destroy our own physical beings in this dynamic.

~ 17 ~

REFERENCES

ACLU (n.d.). *The school to prison pipeline.* https://www.aclu/org/issues/juvenile-justice/school-prison-pipeline.

Adams, D.W. (1995). *Education for extinction: American Indians and the boarding school experience 1875-1928.* University of Kansas Press.

Adams, P. (2009, June 25) Keynote speech given at the *Alternative Education Resource Organization's annual meeting*, Albany, New York.

Addams, J. (1925). Child labor and pauperism. In Johnsen, *Selected articles on child labor.* (pp. 58-59). H. W. Wilson Company.

Alder, J., Fink, N., Bitzer, J., Hosli, I., & Holzgreve, W. (2007). Depression and anxiety during pregnancy: A risk factor for obstetric, fetal and neonatal outcome? A critical review of the literature. *Journal of Maternal- Fetal and Neonatal Medicine, 20,* 189–209.

Alexander KL, Entwisle DR, Kabbini NS. (2001). *The dropout process in life course perspective: Early risk factors at home and school.* Teachers College Record, 103, 760–882.

Alim, T.N., Graves, E., Mellman, T.A., Aigbogun, N., Gray, E., Lawson, W., & Charney, D.S., (2006). Trauma exposure, post-traumatic stress disorder and depression in an African-American primary care population. *Journal of the National Medical Association, 98*(10), 1630-1636. https://www.ncbi.nlm.nih.gov/pmc/articles/PMC2569763/

American Psychiatric Association (2013). *Diagnostic and Statistical Manual of Mental Disorders.* (5th edition). American Psychiatric Publishing.

American Psychological Association (2012). *Suicide among Asian-Americans.* https://www.apa.org/pi/oema/resources/ethnicity-health/asian-american/suicide.

Ames, E. (1997). *The development of Romanian orphan-age children adopted to Canada.* Final report to the National Welfare Grants Program: Human Resources Development Canada. Simon Fraser University.

Ayittey, G.B. (1991). *Indigenous African institutions.* Transnational Publishers.

Bernays, E. (1928). *Propaganda.* Ig Publishing.

Beveridge, A. J. (1907). Child labor and the nation. In *National Child Labor Committee, Child labor and the republic* (p. 118). American Academy of Political and Social Science.

Bird, A. (2007). Perceptions of epigenetics. *Nature, 447,* 396–398.

Blair, R.J., White, S.F., Meffert, H., Hwang, S. (2014). Disruptive behavior disorders: Taking an RDoC(ish) approach. *Current Topics in Behavioral Neuroscience, 16,* 319–336.

Bohm, D. (1980). *Wholeness and the implicate order.* Routledge Classics.

Bonchay, B. (2018). *Narcissistic Abuse Affects Over 158 Million People in the U.S.,* PsychCentral. https://psychcentral.com/lib/narcissistic-abuse-affects-over-158-million-people-in-the-u-s/

Borge, C. (2007, April 27). *Basic instincts: The science of evil.* ABC News. https://abcnews.go.com/Primetime/story?id=2765416&page=1

Boston Children's Hospital. (2018, September 27). When neglected children become adolescents: Study of children in Romanian orphanages tells cautionary tale about family separation. *Science Daily.* https://www.sciencedaily.com/releases/2018/09/180927145549.htm

Bracho, F. (2006). Happiness and indigenous wisdom in the history of the Americas. In Four Arrows, *Unlearning the language of conquest,* (pp. 29–43).

Bright, M.A., Lynne, S.D., Masyn, K.E., Waldman, M.R., Graber, J., & Alexander, R. (2019). Association of Friday school report card release with Saturday incidence rates of agency-verified

physical child abuse. *JAMA Pediatrics. 173*(2). 176-182.
doi:10.1001/jamapediatrics.2018.4346.

Brown, S. (2010). *60 Million Persons in the U.S. Negatively Affected by Someone Else's Pathology.* Psychology Today.
https://www.psychologytoday.com/intl/blog/pathological-relationships/201008/60-million-people-in-the-us-negatively-affected-someone-elses

Burra, N., Kerzel, D., Munoz Tord, D., Grandjean, D., & Ceravolo, L. (2019). Early spatial attention deployment toward and away from aggressive voices, *Social Cognitive and Affective Neuroscience, 14*(1), 73–80, https://doi.org/10.1093/scan/nsy100

Cacioppo, J. (2013). *The lethality of loneliness.* TEDxDesMoines. https://youtu.be/_0hxl03JoA0

Cajete, G. (1994). *Look to the mountain: An ecology of indigenous education.* Kivaki Press.

Cajete, G. (1999). The making of an indigenous teacher: Insights into the ecology of teaching. In J. Kane (Ed.), *Education, information and transformation: Essays on learning and thinking.* (pp. 161-183). Prentice Hall.

Cameron, C.D., Hutcherson, C.A., Ferguson, A.M., Scheffer, J.A., Hadjiandreou, E., and Inzlicht, M. (2019, June). Empathy is hard work: People choose to avoid empathy because of its cognitive costs. *Journal of Experimental Psychology: General 148*(6), 962-976.

Campbell, S., Marriott, M., Nahmias, C., & MacQueen, G. M. (2004). Lower hippocampal volume in patients suffering from depression: A meta-analysis. *American Journal of Psychiatry, 161,* 598–607.

Carnegie Corp. (1986). A Nation Prepared: Teachers for the 21st Century. *The Report of the Task Force on Teaching as a Profession.* Carnegie Corp.

Carrion, V., Haas, B., Garrett, A., Song, S., & Reiss, A. (2009). Reduced Hippocampal Activity in Youth with Posttraumatic Stress Symptoms: An fMRI Study. *Journal of Pediatric Psychology. 35,* 559-69. 10.1093/jpepsy/jsp112.

Caskey, M.M. Ph.D., Rapida, T.J. Ph.D, Wubbold, M. (2001, October 1). *Iroquois confederacy and the US constitution.* Graduate School of Education, Portland State University. http://www.iroquoisdemocracy.pdx.edu/index.htm

Centers for Disease Control and Prevention (2011). *Injury prevention and control: Violence prevention.* http://www.cdc.gov/ViolencePrevention/youthviolence/schoolviolence/index.html

Centers for Disease Control and Prevention (2019, October 15). *Data and statistics about ADHD.* https://www.cdc.gov/ncbddd/adhd/data.html

Center on the Developing Child. (2020). *Toxic Stress.* Harvard University. https://developingchild.harvard.edu/science/key-concepts/toxic-stress/

Cerqueira, J. J., Pego, J. M., Taipa, R., Bessa, J. M., Almeida, O. F. X., & Sousa, N. (2005). Morphological correlates of corticosteroid-induced changes in prefrontal cortex-dependent behaviors. *Journal of Neuroscience, 25,* 7792–7800.

Chang, D.J. & Debiec, J. (2016). Neural correlates of the mother-to-infant social transmission of fear. *Journal of Neuroscience Research, 94*(6), 526-534. https://doi.org/10.1002/jnr.23739.

Chen, G. (2018). *When Teachers Cheat: The Standardized Test Controversies.* Public School Review. https://www.publicschoolreview.com/blog/when-teachers-cheat-the-standardized-test-controversies

Child, B.J. (2000). *Boarding school seasons: American Indian families, 1900-1940.* University of Nebraska Press.

Child Trends Bank (2010). *High school dropout rates.* http://www.childtrendsdatabank.org/

Chomsky, N., (2002). *Understanding power: The indispensable Chomsky.* The New York Press.

Christov-Moore, L., Sugiyama, T., Grigaityte, K., and Iacoboni, M. (2017b). Increasing generosity by disrupting prefrontal cortex. *Society for Neuroscience. 12,* 174–181. doi: 10.1080/17470919.2016.1154105

Christov-Moore, L., and Iacoboni, M. (2016). Self-other resonance, its control and prosocial inclinations: brain-behavior relationships. *Human Brain Mapping. 37*, 1544–1558. doi: 10.1002/hbm.23119

Coenen, D. T. (2004). *Constitutional law: the Commerce Clause.* Foundation Press.

Cole, S. W., Hawkley, L. C., Arevalo, J. M., Sung, C. Y., Rose, R. M., & Cacioppo, J. T. (2007). Social regulation of gene expression in human leukocytes. *Genome Biology, 8*, R189.1–R189.13.

Constantinidis, C. & Luna, B. (2019). Neural substrates of inhibitory control maturation in adolescence. *Trends in Neurosciences, 42*(9), 604-616. doi:10.1016/j.tins.2019.07.004

Copeland, W.E., Shanahan, L., Hinesley, J., Chan, R.F., Aberg, K.A., Fairbank, J.A., van den Oord, E.J.C.G., & Costello, E.J. (2018). Association of childhood trauma exposure with adult psychiatric disorders and functional outcomes. *JAMA Network Open, 1.* doi:10.1001/jamanetworkopen.2018.4493

Dahoun, T., Nour, M.M., McCutcheon, R.A., Adams, R.A., Bloomfield, M.A., & Howes, O.D. (2019). The relationship between childhood trauma, dopamine release and dexamphetamine-induced positive psychotic symptoms: a [11C]-(+)-PHNO PET study. *Translational Psychiatry, 9*(287). 1-12.

Daftary, S, Van Enkevor, E., Kulikova, A., Legacy, M. & Brown, E.S. (2019). Relationship between depressive symptom severity and amygdala volume in a large community-based sample. *Psychiatry Research: Neuroimaging 283*, 77-82.

Dalton, K. M., Nacewicz, B. M., Alexander, A. L., & Davidson, R. J. (2007). Gaze-fixation, brain activation, and amygdala volume in unaffected siblings of individuals with autism. *Biological Psychiatry, 61*, 512–520.

Dalton, K. M., Nacewicz, B. M., Johnstone, T., Schaefer, H. S., Gernsbacher, M. A., Goldsmith, H. H., Davidson, R. J. (2005). Gaze fixation and the neural circuitry of face processing in autism. *Nature Neuroscience, 8*, 519–526.

Darwin, C. (1871). *The descent of man, and selection in relation to sex.* London.

Dashtestani, H., Zaragoza, R., Kermanian, R., Knutson, K.M., Halem, M., Casey, A., Karamzadeh, N.S., Anderson, A.A., Boccara, A.C., & Gandjbakhche, A. (2018).The role of prefrontal cortex in a moral judgment task using functional near-infrared spectroscopy. *Brain and Behavior, 8*(11) https://doi.org/10.1002/brb3.1116

Davies, E. T. (1907). The enforcement of child labor legislation in Illinois. in *National Child Labor Committee, Child labor and the republic.* American Academy of Political and Social Science, New York.

Dewey, J. 1988 (1939). Experience, knowledge and value: a rejoinder. In JA. Boyston, (ed.), John Dewey. *The later works. 1925 - 1953. Volume 14: 1939-1941,* (pp. 3-90). Southern Illinois University Press.

Dewey, J. (1910). *How we think.* Dover Publications.

Dewey, J. (1897). My pedagogic creed. *School Journal 54*, (pp. 77-80).

Dewey, J. (1915). *The school and society*. The University of Chicago Press.

DiPietro, J. A. (2009). Psychological and psychophysiological considerations on the maternal–fetal relationship. *Infant & Child Development*, DOI: 10.1002/icd.651.

Domjan, M. (2005). Pavlovian conditioning: A functional perspective. *Annual Review of Psychology, 56*, 179 -206.

D'Onofrio, B., Emery, R. (2019). Parental divorce or separation and children's mental health. *World Psychiatry, 18*(1), 100-101. doi:10.1002/wps.20590

Drozak, J. & Bryla, J. (2005). Dopamine: Not just a neurotransmitter. *PubMed 59*, 405-420. https://www.ncbi.nlm.nih.gov/pubmed/16106242

Edwards, C. (1989). Self-regulation: The key to motivating at-risk children. *The Clearing House, 63*(2), 59- 62.

Edwards, C. (1993). *Classroom discipline and management*. Macmillan College.

Edwards, C. (1994). Learning and control in the classroom. *Journal of Instructional Psychology, 21*(4), 340-346.

Elfman, L. (2010). *Texas state board of education approves controversial social studies curriculum changes*. Diverse Education. http://diverseeducation.com/article/13821/

Ellis, B.H., Fisher, P.A., & Zaharie, S. (2004). Predictors of disruptive behavior, developmental delays, anxiety, and affective symptomatology among institutionally reared Romanian children. *Journal of the American Academy of Child and Adolescent Psychiatry, 43*(10), 1283–1292.

Encyclopedia Britannica Online (2018). *Frederick II: king of Prussia.* https://www.britannica.com/biography/Frederick-II-king-of-Prussia

Fafunwa, A. B. (1974). *A history of education in Nigeria.* Allen & Unwin.

Fair Test (2007). *How standardized testing damages education.* http://fairtest.org/how-standardized-testing-damages-education-pdf.

Fales, C. L., Barch, D. M., Rundle, M. M., Mintun, M. A., Snyder, A. Z., Cohen, J. D., Sheline, Y. I. (2008). Altered emotional interference processing in affective and cognitive-control brain circuitry in major depression. *Biological Psychiatry, 63*, 377–384.

Farland, S. (2018). *Report Card shows little gain in U.S. students' math, reading scores.* UPI. https://www.upi.com/Top_News/US/2018/04/10/Report-Card-shows-little-gain-in-US-students-math-reading-scores/6531523372207/.

Felt, J. P. (1965). *Hostages of fortune: child labor reform in New York State.* Syracuse University Press.

Fertig, B. (2010, November). *N.Y. Mayor wins waiver for schools chancellor pick.* NPR online http://www.npr.org/2010/11/30/

131687228/bloomberg-wins-waiver-for-schools-chancellor-pick

Forbes, J. (1979). Traditional Native American philosophy and multicultural education. In *Multicultural education and the American Indian* (pp. 3-13). Los Angeles: American Indian Studies Center, University of California.

Forbes, Scott H. (2003). *Holistic education: An analysis of its ideas and nature.* Foundation for Educational Renewal.

Freire, P. (1970). *Pedagogy of the oppressed.* New York: Continuum International Publishing Group, Inc.

Gangrade, A. (2012). The effect of music on the production of neurotransmitters, hormones, cytokines, and peptides: A review. *Music and Medicine, 4*, 40-43. 10.1177/1943862111415117.

Ganzel, B., Kim, P., Glover, G., & Temple, E. (2008). Resilience after 9/11: Multimodal neuroimaging evidence for stress-related change in the healthy adult brain. *NeuroImage, 40*, 788–795.

Ganzel, B. L., Morris, P. A., & Wethington, E. (2010). Allostasis and the human brain: Integrating models of stress from the social and life sciences. *Psychological Review, 117*(1), 134–174. http://doi.org/10.1037/a0017773

Gatto, J.T. (2008, October). "Childhood's end," Ode magazine edited excerpt from Weapons of Mass Instruction: A schoolteacher's journey through the dark world of compulsory schooling, *New Society Publishers, 6*(8), 23-25.

Gatto, J.T. (1992) *Dumbing us down: The hidden curriculum of compulsory schooling.* New Society Publishers.

Gatto, J.T. (2009, September) Take back your education. *Yes! magazine.* http://www.yesmagazine.org/issues/learn-as-you-go/take-back-your-education

Gatto, J.T. (2001). *The history of American education: A school-teacher'30s intimate investigation into the problem of modern schooling.* Oxford Village Press.

Geidd, J., M.d. (2014). *Inside the teenage Brain,* PBS Frontline. https://www.pbs.org/wgbh/pages/frontline/shows/teen-brain/interviews/giedd.html

Gibbons, C.E. (1925). Extent and control of rural child labor. In Johnsen, *Selected articles on child labor.* H. W. Wilson Company.

Giroux, H.A. (2010). Governing Through Crime and the Pedagogy of Punishment. In *Education as enforcement: The militarization and corporatization of schooling.* Routledge.

Gopnik, A. (1996). The scientist as child. *Philosophy of Science, 63*(4), 485.514.

Gray, P. (2011). *Psychology* (6th edition). Worth Publishers.

Greene, J. D., Nystrom, L. E., Engell, A. D., Darley, J. M., & Cohen, J. D. (2004). The neural bases of cognitive conflict and control in moral judgment. *Neuron, 44*(2), 389–400. https://doi.org/10.1016/j.neuron.2004.09.027

Greene, J. D., Sommerville, R. B., Nystrom, L. E., Darley, J. M., & Cohen, J. D. (2001). An fMRI investigation of emotional engagement in moral judgment. *Science, 293*(5537), 2105–2108. https://doi.org/10.1126/science.1062872

Groome, L. J., Swiber, M. J., Bentz, L. S., Holland, S. B., & Atterbury, J. L. (1995). Maternal anxiety during pregnancy: Effect on fetal behavior at 38 and 40 weeks of gestation. *Journal of Developmental and Behavioral Pediatrics, 16*, 391–396.

Haines Mofford, J. (1997). *Child labor in America.* Discovery Enterprises. p. 42.

Hamilton, J. (2014). *Orphans' lonely beginnings reveal how parents shape a child's brain.* NPR Morning Edition. https://www.npr.org/sections/health-shots/2014/02/20/280237833/orphans-lonely-beginnings-reveal-how-parents-shape-a-childs-brain

Han, H., Chen, J., Jeong, C., & Glover, G. H. (2016). Influence of the cortical midline structures on moral emotion and motivation in moral decision-making. *Behavioural Brain Research, 302*, 237–251. https://doi.org/10.1016/j.bbr.2016.01.001

Han, H., Glover, G. H., & Jeong, C. (2014). Cultural influences on the neural correlate of moral decision making processes. *Behavioural Brain Research, 259*, 215–228. https://doi.org/10.1016/j.bbr.2013.11.012

Hare, J. (2010). *Holistic education: An interpretation for teachers in the IB programmes.* International Baccalaureate Organization.

Hare, R.D., Neumann, C.S. (2008). Psychopathy as a clinical and empirical construct. *Annual Review of Clinical Psychology 4*, 217–246.

Harper, L.V. (2005). Epigenetic inheritance and the intergenerational transfer of experience. University of California, Davis: Psychological Bulletin. *American Psychological Association, 131*(3), 340-360.

Harrison, S (2002). *The happy child.* Sentient Publications.

Hindman, H.D. (2002). *Child labor: an American history.* M.E. Sharp.

Hobsbawm, E. J. (1999). *Industry and empire: The birth of the industrial revolution.* The New Press.

Hodges, J., & Tizard, B. (1989). Social and family relationships of ex-institutional adolescents. *Journal of Child Psychology and Psychiatry, 30* (1), 77–97.

Holt, J. (1964) *How children fail.* Pitman Publishing Corporation.

Howie, L.D., Pastor, P.N., Lukacs, S.L. (2014, April). Use of medication prescribed for emotional or behavioral difficulties among children aged 6-17 years in the United States, 2011-2012. *NCHS Data Brief*, 148, 1-8. ncbi.nlm.nih.gov/pubmed/24762418

Huecker, M.R. & Smock, W. (2019). *Domestic Violence.* StatPearls Publishing.

Inglis, A. (1918). *Principles of secondary education.* Houghton Mifflin Company, Harvard University.

Jablonka, E., & Lamb, M. J. (1995). *Epigenetic inheritance and evolution.* Oxford University Press.

Jablonka, E., & Raz, G. (2009). Transgenerational epigenetic inheritance: Prevalence, mechanisms, and implications for the study of heredity and evolution. *The Quarterly Review of Biology, 84,* 131–176.

Jacobs, D. (2003) Forced Hegemony: Warnings and Solutions from Indian Country. In Gabbard, D. (Ed.) *Education as enforcement: The militarization and corporatization of schooling.* RoutledgeFalmer.

Jacobs, D.T. (1998). *Primal awareness.* Inner Traditions.

James, F. (2010). *Arizona governor signs ethnic-studies ban.* National Public Radio. http://www.npr.org/blogs/thetwo-way/2010/05/arizona_gov_signs_ethnicstudie.html

Joffe, J. M. (1969). Prenatal determinants of behaviour. In H. J. Eysenck (General ed.) *International series of monographs in experimental psychology, 7.* Pergamon.

Johnson, D.E. (2002). Adoption and the effect on children's development. *Early Human Development, 68* (1), 39–54.

Jonathan, H. (2003). The moral emotions. In R. J. Davidson, K. Scherer, & H. H. Goldsmith (Eds.), *Handbook of affective sciences,* (pp. 852–870). Oxford University Press.

Kaati, G., Bygren, L. O., & Edvinsson, S. (2002). Cardiovascular and diabetes mortality determined by nutrition during parents' and grandparents' slow growth period. *European Journal of Human Genetics, 10*, 682– 688.

Kasenbacher, M. (2012, December 24). *Work, learning and freedom: Interview with Noam Chomsky.* New Left Project. https://chomsky.info/20121224/

Keltner, D. (2016, October). Don't let power corrupt you. *Harvard Business Review*, 108-111.

Kessler, R., Sonnega, A., Bromet, E., Hughes, M., & Nelson, C. (1995). Post-traumatic stress disorder in the National Comorbidity Study. *Archives of General Psychiatry, 52*, 1048–1059.

Klein, R. & Preston, C. (2018). *When schools use child protective services as a weapon against parents.* The Hechinger Report. https://hechingerreport.org/when-schools-use-child-protective-services-as-a-weapon-against-parents/.

Knutsen, R., Filippov, V., Knutsen, S.F., Fraser, G.E., Lloren, J., Juma, D., & Duerksen-Hughes, P. (2019). Cold parenting is associated with cellular aging in offspring: A retrospective study. *Biological Psychology, 145*,142-149. https://doi.org/10.1016/j.biopsycho.2019.03.013.

Koen, B., Viding, E., Muetzel, R.L., El Marroun, H., Kocevska, D., White, T., Tiemeier, H., & Cecil, C.A.M. (2018). Neural profile of callous traits in children: A population-based neuroimaging study. *Biological Psychiatry, 85*(5), 399-407.https://doi.org/10.1016/j.biopsych.2018.10.015

Koenigs, M., Young, L., Adolphs, R., Tranel, D., Cushman, F., Hauser, M., & Damasio, A. (2007). Damage to the prefrontal cortex increases utilitarian moral judgements. *Nature, 446*(7138), 908. https://doi.org/10.1038/nature05631

Kornblith, G.J. (1997). *The industrial revolution in America; Problems in American civilization.* Wadsworth Publishing.

Kraus, M.W., Côté, S., Keltner, D. (2010). Social class, contextualism, and empathic accuracy. *Psychological Science, 21*(11).

Kridel, C.A. (ed.) (2010). *Encyclopedia of curriculum studies, vol. 2.* University of South Carolina: Sage Reference.

La Buissonnière-Ariza, V., Séguin, J.R., Nassim, M., Boivin,M., Pine, D.S., Lepore, F., Tremblay, R.E., & Maheu, F.S.. (2019). Chronic harsh parenting and anxiety associations with fear circuitry function in healthy adolescents: A preliminary study, *Biological Psychology 145,* 198-210. DOI: 10.1016/j.biopsycho.2019.03.019

Lenin, V. (1914). *Karl Marx: A brief biographical sketch.* http://www.marxists.org/archive/lenin/works/1914/granat/ch01.htm#fwV21E029

Levine, B.E. (2018). *Resisting Illegitimate Authority:A Thinking Person's Guide to Being an Anti- Authoritarian—Strategies, Tools, and Models.* AK Press.

Lewey, G. (2004). *Were American Indians the victims of genocide?* George Mason University's History News Network, http://hnn.us/articles/7302.html.

Lewis, D.R. (1995). Native Americans and the environment: A survey of twentieth century issues. *American Indian Quarterly, 19*, 423-450. University of Nebraska Press.

Lindenmeyer, K. (1997). *A right to childhood: the U.S. Children's Bureau and child welfare, 1912-46.* University of Illinois Press.

Lindsey, D. (2018, August). Calling out phony philanthropists. *The Chronicle of Philanthropy.* https://www.philanthropy.com/article/Calling-Out-Phony/244373

Lovejoy, O. (1907). Child labor in the soft coal mines. In *National Child Labor Committee, Child labor and the republic.* American Academy of Political and Social Science.

Lumey, L. H., & Stein, A. D. (1997). Offspring birth weights after maternal intrauterine undernutrition: A comparison within sibships. *American Journal of Epidemiology, 146*, 810–819.

Mallon, H.W. (2019). *When mindfulness is a trauma trigger: April #MeToo.* ACES Connection. https://www.acesconnection.com/blog/when-mindfulness-is-a-trauma-trigger-april-metoo

Masterpasqua, F. (2009). Psychology and epigenetics. *Review of General Psychology, 13*(3), 194-201, American Psychological Association.

Mathison, S. and Ross, E.W. (eds.) (2004). The nature and limits of standards-based reform and assessment. *Defending public schools, Volume IV.* Praeger Perspectives.

McCune Lindsay, S. (1907). Child labor and the public schools. In *National Child Labor Committee, Child labor and the republic.* American Academy of Political and Social Science.

McDonald, K. (2018). *How school districts weaponize child protection services against uncooperative parents.* Foundation for Economic Education. https://fee.org/articles/how-school-districts-weaponize-child-protection-services-against-uncooperative-parents

McDonald, K. (2018). *Harvard study shows the dangers of early school enrollment.* Foundation for Economic Education. https://fee.org/articles/harvard-study-shows-the-dangers-of-early-school-enrollment

McGowan, P. O., Sasaki, A., D'Alessio, A. C., Dymov, S., Labonté, B., Szyf, M., Turecki, G., & Meaney, M. J. (2009). Epigenetic regulation of the glucocorticoid receptor in human brain associates with childhood abuse. *Nature Neuroscience, 12*(3), 342–348. https://doi.org/10.1038/nn.2270

Meaney, M. J. (2001). Maternal care, gene expression, and the transmission of individual differences in stress reactivity across generations. *Annual Review of Neuroscience, 24,* 1161–1192.

Meaney, M. (2004). The nature of nurture: Maternal effects and chromatin remodeling. In J. T. Cacioppo & G. G. Berntson (Eds.), *Essays in social neuroscience.* MIT Press.

Meaney, M. J., Szyf, M., & Seckl, J. R. (2007). Epigenetic mechanisms of perinatal programming of hypothalamic-pituitary-adrenal function and health. *Trends in Molecular Medicine, 13,* 269-277.

Mei, L., Zhibing, T., Robinson, H.L., Yin, D.M., Liu, Y., Liu, F., Wang, H., Lin, T.W., Xing, G., Gan, L., & Xiong, W.C. (2018). Dynamic ErbB4 activity in hippocampal-prefrontal synchrony and top-down attention in rodents. *Neuron, 98*(2) 380-393.

Mendizza, M. (2009). *Everything we think about school is wrong: An interview with John Taylor Gatto.* Touch the Future. https://ttfuture.org/blog/michael/everything-we-think-about-schooling-wrong-interview-john-taylor-gatto

Mennes, M., Van den Bergh, B. R. H., Lagae, L., & Stiers, P. (2009). Developmental brain alterations in 17 year old boys are related to antenatal maternal anxiety. *Clinical Neurophysiology, 120*(6), 1116–1122.

Mezerow, J. (1991). *Transformative dimensions of adult learning.* Josey-Bass.

Milgram, S. (1963). Behavioral study of obedience. *Journal of Abnormal and Social Psychology, 67,* 371-378.

Milgram, S. (1974). *Obedience to authority: An experimental view.* HarperCollins.

Milgram, S. (1973, December). The perils of obedience. *Harper's Magazine,* 62-77.

Mill, P., & Petronis, A. (2008). Pre- and peri-natal environmental risks for attention-deficit hyperactivity disorder (ADHD): The potential role of epigenetic processes in mediating sus-

ceptibility. *Journal of Child Psychology and Psychiatry, 49,*
1020–1030.

Miller, C. (2020). *How trauma affects kids in school.* Child Mind
Institute. https://childmind.org/article/how-trauma-affects-
kids-school/.

Miller, R. (1997). *What are schools for? Holistic education in American culture.* Holistic Education Press.

Miller, W. E. (1907). The child labor situation in Ohio and bor-
der states. In *National Child Labor Committee, Child labor and the
republic.* American Academy of Political and Social Science.

Mock, S. E., & Arai, S. M. (2011). Childhood trauma and
chronic illness in adulthood: mental health and socioeconomic status as explanatory factors and buffers. *Frontiers in
psychology, 1,* 246. https://doi.org/10.3389/fpsyg.2010.00246

Moffitt, T. E., Caspi, A., & Rutter, M. (2006). Measured gene-en-
vironment interactions in psychopathology: Concepts, research strategies, and implications for research, intervention,
and public understanding of genetics. *Perspectives on Psychological Science, 1,* 5–27.

Moller, J., Brackett, M.A., Ivcevic, Z., & White, A.E. (2020,
April). High school students' feelings: Discoveries from a large
national survey and an experience sampling study. *Learning
and Instruction; 66.* https://doi.org/10.1016/j.learnin-
struc.2019.101301

Mollov, B., Mudahogora, C., & Shrira, A. (2019). Complex PTSD and intergenerational transmission of distress and resilience among Tutsi genocide survivors and their offspring: A preliminary report. *Psychiatry Research, 271*, 121 DOI: 10.1016/j.psychres.2018.11.040

Mosley, W. (2018). Walter Mosley: Enough with the victors writing history. Literary Hub. https://lithub.com/walter-mosley-enough-with-the-victors-writing-history/

Moumouni, A. (1968). *Education in Africa.* New York: Praeger.

Naish, K.R. & Obhi, S.S. (2015). Self-selected conscious strategies do not modulate motor cortical output during action observation. *Journal of Neuropsychology 114*(4), 2278 –2284. https://doi.org/10.1152/jn.00518.2015

National Assessment of Educational Progress data, (2007). http://nces.ed.gov/nationsreportcard/ ; http://nces.ed.gov/programs/digest/d08/tables/dt08_118.asp?referrer=list ; http://nces.ed.gov/programs/digest/d08/tables/dt08_116.asp?referrer=list

NAEP. (2015). The nation's report card. *Department of Education, Institute of Education Sciences*, National Center for Education Statistics.

National Center for Education Statistics (1993). *20 Years of American education: A statistical portrait.* Edited by Tom Snyder. https://nces.ed.gov/naal/lit_history.asp

National Center for Education Statistics (2008). *Labor force status of high school dropouts, by sex and race/ethnicity: Selected years, 1980 through 2007.* http://nces.ed.gov/programs/digest/d08/tables/dt08_389.asp

National Center for Education Statistics (2019). *PIAAC results.* https://www.cdc.gov/ncbddd/adhd/data.html

National Center for Health Statistics. (2014). *Health, United States, 2013: With Special Feature on Prescription Drugs.* http://www.cdc.gov/nchs/hus.htm

National Commission on Teaching and America's Future. (1996). *What matters most: Teaching for America's future.* NCTAF.

Nearing, S. (1925). Social cost of child Labor. In Johnsen, *Selected articles on child labor,* (p. 65). H. W. Wilson Company.

Neigh, G.N., Gillespie, C. F., & Nemeroff, C. B. (2009). The neurobiological toll of child abuse and neglect. *Trauma, Violence, and Abuse 10*(4), 389-410.

Nesse, R. (2019). *Good Reasons for Bad Feelings: Insights from the frontier of evolutionary psychiatry.* Penguin Random House, LLC.

Oberlander, T. F., Weinberg, J., Papsdorf, M., Grunau, R., Misri, S., & Devlin, A. M. (2008). Prenatal exposure to maternal depression, neonatal methylation of human glucocorticoid receptor gene (NR3C1) and infant corti- sol stress responses. *Epigenetics, 3,* 97-106.

Ohashi, K., Anderson, C.M., Bolger, E.A., Khan, A., McGreenery, C.E., & Teicher, M.H., (2018). Susceptibility or Resilience to

Maltreatment Can Be Explained by Specific Differences in Brain Network Architecture, *Biological Psychiatry 85*(8), 690-702. DOI: 10.1016/j.biopsych.2018.10.016

Okeke, A. (1982). Traditional education in Igboland. In f. Ogbalu & E. Emenanjo (Eds.), *Igbo language and culture, 2*, 15-26. Ibadan University Press.

Owen, D. & Davidson, J. (2009, May). Hubris syndrome: An acquired personality disorder? A study of US Presidents and UK Prime Ministers over the last 100 years. *Brain, a Journal of Neurology, 132*(5), 1396-1406.

Pavlov, I. P. (1926). *Conditioned reflexes and psychiatry: Lectures on conditioned reflexes, Vol. 2*. Read Books Limited (2013).

Pembrey, M. E., Bygren, L. O., Kaati, G., Edvinsson, S., Northstone, K., Sjöström, M., et al. (2006). Sex-specific, male-line transgenerational responses in humans. *European Journal of Human Genetics, 14*, 159– 166.

Philips, S.U. (1983). *The invisible culture: Communication in classroom and community on the Warm Springs Indian Reservation*. Waveland Press, Inc.

Pinto, M. (2019). *Only a Teacher*. PBS. https://www.pbs.org/onlyateacher/timeline.html

Pleis, J.R., and Lethbridge-Çejku, M. (2006). Summary health statistics for U.S. adults: National health interview survey, 2005. *Vital Health Stat, 10*(232). National Center for Health Statistics.

Pratt, R.H. (1964). *Battlefield and classroom: Four decades with the American Indian, 1867-1904.* Utley, R.M. (ed.). Yale University Press.

Pratt, R.H. (1892). The advantages of mingling Indians with Whites, *Proceedings of the National Conference of Charities and Correction, 1895. 2,* 5.

Pray, L. A. (2006). Epigenetics: Genome, meet your environment. *Scientist, 18*(13), 14–20.

Prehn, K., Wartenburger, I., Mériau, K., Scheibe, C., Goodenough, O. R., Villringer, A., Heekeren, H. R. (2007). Individual differences in moral judgment competence influence neural correlates of socio-normative judgments. *Social Cognitive and Affective Neuroscience, 3*(1), 33–46. https://doi.org/10.1093/scan/nsm037

Quinlan, E.B., Barker, E.D., Luo, Q., Banaschewski, T., Bokde, A.L.W., Bromberg, U., Büchel, C., Desrivières, S., Flor, H., Frouin, V., Garavan, H., Chaarani, B., Gowland, P., Heinz, A., Brühl, R., Martinot, J.L., Martinot, M.L.P. Nees, F., Orfanos, D.P., Paus,T., Poustka, L. Hohmann, S., Smolka, M.N., Fröhner, J.H., Walter, H., Whelan, R., Schumann G. & IMAGEN Consortium (2018). Peer victimization and its impact on adolescent brain development and psychopathology. *Molecular Psychiatry.* https://doi.org/10.1038/s41380-018-0297-9

Quinn, D. (1999). *Beyond civilization.* Three Rivers Press.

Quinn, D. (1992). *Ishmael.* Bantam/Turner Book.

Race to the Top (2010). *Obama White House* Https://oba-mawhitehouse.archives.gov/issues/education/k-12/race-to-the-top

Rakyan, V. K., & Beck, S. (2006). Epigenetic variation and inheritance in mammals. *Current Opinion in Genetics and Development, 16*, 573–577.

Reagan, T. (2005). *Non-western educational traditions; Indigenous approaches to educational thought and practice,* (3rd Edition). Lawrence Erlbaum Associates.

Richards, E. J. (2006). Inherited epigenetic variation: Revisiting soft inheritance. *Nature Reviews Genetics, 7*, 395–401.

Richards, J.S., Cohen, J.S., & Chavis, L. (2019). *The quiet rooms.* Pro Publica. https://features.propublica.org/illinois-seclusion-rooms/school-students-put-in-isolated-timeouts/

Rimfeld, K., Malanchini, M., Kraphl, E., Hannigan, L.J., Dale, P.S., & Plomin, R (2018). The stability of educational achievement across school years is largely explained by genetic factors. npj *Science of Learning 3*, 16. https://www.nature.com/articles/s41539-018-0030-0

Rosenberg, C.M. (2013) *Child labor in America: a history.* McFarland & Company Inc.

Rossiter, M.C. (1996). Incidence and consequences of inherited environmental effects. *Annual Review of Ecology and Systematics, 27*(1), 451-476.

Rutowski, L. (2001). Contradictions of school reform: Educational costs of standardized testing. Linda McNeil (ed). *Journal of Educational Change*, 2(1), 75-78.

Sable, J., Gaviola, N. (December, 2007). Numbers and rates of public high school dropouts: school year 2004-05, *U.S. Department of Education NCES* 2008-305, National Center for Educational Statistics, Institute of Educational Sciences; http://nces.ed.gov/pubs2008/2008305.pdf

Sallee, S. (2004). *The whiteness of child labor reform in the New South*. University of Georgia Press.

Saltman, K, and Gabbard, D. (eds.) (2011). *Education as enforcement: The militarization and corporatization of schools*, (2nd Edition). Forward by Giroux, H., New York: Routledge.

Schmidt, J. D. (2010). *Industrial violence and the legal origins of child labor*. Cambridge University Press.

Shanab, M. E., & Yahya, K. A. (1978). A cross-cultural study of obedience. *Bulletin of the Psychonomic Society*.

Sheline, Y. I. (2003). Neuroimaging studies of mood disorder effects on the brain. *Biological Psychiatry, 54*, 338–352.

Sheline, Y. I., Barch, D. M., Donnelly, J. M., Ollinger, J. M., Snyder, A. Z., & Mintun, M. A. (2001). Increased amygdala response to masked emotional faces in depressed subjects resolves with antidepressant treatment: An fMRI study. *Biological Psychiatry, 50*, 651–658.

Sheline, Y. I., Gado, M. H., & Price, J. L. (1998). Amygdala core nuclei volumes are decreased in recurrent major depression. *NeuroReport, 9*, 2023–2028.

Sjöström, K., Valentin, L., Thelin, T., & Marsal, K. (2002). Maternal anxiety in late pregnancy: Effect on fetal movements and fetal heart rate. *Early Human Development, 67*, 87–100.

Slattery, P. (2006). *Curriculum development in the postmodern era* (2nd Edition). Routledge, Taylor & Francis Group.

Smith, P. B., and Bond, M. H. (1998). *Social psychology across cultures*, (2nd Edition). Prentice Hall.

Smith. P.S. (2006). The effects of solitary confinement on prison inmates: A brief history and review of the literature. *Crime and Justice, 34*, 1, 441-528. University of Chicago Press.

Smyke, A.T., Koga, S.F., Johnson, D.E., Fox, N.A., Marshall, P.J., Nelson, C.A., Zeanah, C.H., & Group, B.C. (2007). The caregiving context in institution-reared and family-reared infants and toddlers in Romania. *Journal of Child Psychology and Psychiatry, 48*(2), 210–218.

Spinoza, B. (1669). *Tractate Religico Politicu*. Translated by Jonathan Bennett (2017). https://www.earlymodern-texts.com/assets/pdfs/spinoza1669.pdf

Spitz, V. (2005). *Doctors from hell: The horrific account of Nazi experiments on humans*. Sentient Publications.

Spring, J. (1997). *Deculturalization and the struggle for equality: A brief history of the education of dominated cultures in the United States* (2nd Edition). McGraw Hill.

Susser, E., Hoek, H. W., & Brown, A. (1998). Neurodevelopmental disorders after prenatal famine: The story of the Dutch famine study. *American Journal of Epidemiology, 147,* 213–216.

Szyf, M., McGowan, P., & Meaney, M. J. (2008). The social environment and the epigenome. *Environmental and Molecular Mutagenesis, 49,* 46–60.

Talge, N. M., Neal, C., Glover, V., and the early stress translational research and prevention science network (2007). Fetal and neonatal experience on child and adolescent mental health. Antenatal maternal stress and long-term effects on child neurodevelopment: how and why? *Journal of Child Psychology and Psychiatry, 48,* 245–261.

Tang, L., Darlington, G., Ma, D.W.L., Haines, J. and on behalf of the Guelph Family Health Study (2018). Mothers' and fathers' media parenting practices associated with young children's screen-time: a cross-sectional study. *BMC Obesity, 5*(37). https://doi.org/10.1186/s40608-018-0214-4

The New American Academy (2018). *The Prussian Industrial Model.*. https://thenewamericanacademy.wordpress.com/about/our-philosophy/the-prussian-industrial-model/

Thompson, V. (2018). *Do standardized test scores factor into how much money a school will receive?* The Classroom.

https://www.theclassroom.com/standardized-test-scores-factor-much-money-school-receive-25534.html

Todd, H. M. (1925). Why children work. In Johnsen, *Selected articles on child labor*. H. W. Wilson Company, New York.

Tollrain, R. & Harvell, C. D. (ed.) (1999). *The ecology and evolution of inducible defenses*. Princeton University Press.

Tottenham, N. (2015). Social scaffolding of human amygdala-mPFC circuit development. *Social Neuroscience Journal, 10*(5), 489-499. https://doi.org/10.1080/17470919.2015.1087424

Tottenham, N., Hare, T.A., Quinn, B.T., McCarry, T.W., Nurse, M., Gilhooly, T., Millner, A., Galvan, A., Davidson, M.C., Eigsti, I.M., Thomas, K.M., Freed, P.J., Booma, E.S., Gunnar, M.R., Altemus, M., Aronson, J., & Casey, B.J. (2009). Prolonged institutional rearing is associated with atypically large amygdala volume and difficulties in emotion regulation. *The Journal of Analytical Psychology, 13*(1), 46-61. https://onlinelibrary.wiley.com/doi/full/10.1111/j.1467-7687.2009.00852.x

Trattner, W.I. (1970). *Crusade for the children: a history of the National Child Labor Committee and child labor reform in America*, (pp. 28-29).Quadrangle Books.

Treadway, M.T., Cooper, J.A., & Miller, A.H. (2019). Can't or won't? Immunometobolic constraints on dopaminergic drive. *Trends in Cognitive Sciences, 23*(5), 435-448.

Troen, S. K. (1976). The discovery of the adolescent by American educational reformers, 1900–1920: an economic perspective. In *Schooling and Society*, Lawrence Stone, (ed.) (pp. 239-249). Johns Hopkins University Press.

Tsavoussis, A., Stawicki, S.P.A., Stoicea, N., & Papadimos, T.J. (2014). Child-witnessed domestic violence and its adverse effects on brain development: A call for societal self-examination and awareness. *Frontiers in Public Health, 2*, 178. doi: 10.3389/fpubh.2014.00178.

Twenge, J.M., Cooper, A.B., Joiner, T.E., Duffy, M.E., &Binau, S.G. (2019). Age, period, and cohort trends in mood disorder indicators and suicide related outcomes in a nationally representative dataset, 2005–2017. *Journal of Abnormal Psychology, 128*(3), 185-199. https://www.apa.org/pubs/journals/releases/abn-abn0000410.pdf.

Tyack, D. (1975). *The one best system: A history of American urban education*. Harvard University Press.

Tyack, D. and Cuban, L. (1995). *Tinkering toward utopia: A century of public school reform*. Harvard University Press.

Tyack, D. and Hansot, E. (1982). *Managers of virtue: Public school leadership in America, 1821-1980*. Basic Books.

Tyborowska, A., Volman, I., Niermann, H.C.M. et al. (2018). Early-life and pubertal stress differentially modulate grey matter development in human adolescents. *Scientific Reports 8*, 9201. https://doi.org/10.1038/s41598-018-27439-5

Ueda, R., Yanagisawa, K., Ashida, H. & Abe, N. (2018). Executive control and faithfulness: only long-term romantic relationships require prefrontal control. *Experimental Brain Research, 236,* 821–828. https://doi.org/10.1007/s00221-018-5181-y.

United States Department of Labor (2017). History of child labor in the United States - Part 2: The reform movement. *Bureau of Labor Statistics.* https://www.bls.gov/opub/mlr/2017/article/history-of-child-labor-in-the-united-states-part-2-the-reform-movement.htm

U.S. Department of Education (1983). *A Nation at Risk.* https://www2.ed.gov/pubs/NatAtRisk/risk.html

U.S. Department of Education (2009). *High school dropout and completion rates in the United States: 2007.* Compendium report.http://nces.ed.gov/pubs2009/2009064.pdf

U.S. Department of Education, National Center for Education Statistics. (2010). *The Condition of Education 2010* (NCES 2010-028), Table A-19-2.

U.S. Department of Education (2017). *National assessment of educational progress.* https://www.nationsreportcard.gov/math_2017/#?grade=4.

U.S. Department of Labor, Bureau of Labor Statistics (2007). *Tabulations.* http://www.bls.gov/cps/cpsaat7.pd.

U.S. Department of Education (2010). *Race to the top fund.* https://www2.ed.gov/programs/racetothetop/index.html

Van den Bergh, B. R. H. (1990). The influence of maternal emotions during pregnancy on fetal and neonatal behavior. *Pre- and Perinatal Psychology Journal, 5*, 119–130

Van den Bergh, B. R. H. (1992). Maternal emotions during pregnancy and fetal and neonatal behaviour. In J. G. Nijhuis (Ed.), *Fetal behaviour: Developmental and perinatal aspects*, 157–178. Oxford University Press.

Van den Bergh, B. R. H. (2010). Some societal and historical scientific considerations regarding the mother-fetus relationship and parenthood, *Infant and Child Development, 19*(1), 39-44. https://doi.org/10.1002/icd.652

Van den Bergh, B. R. H., Mulder, E. J. H., Visser, G. H. A., Poelmann-Weesjes, G., Bekedam, D. J., & Prechtl, H. F. R. (1989). The effect of (induced) maternal emotions on fetal behaviour: A controlled study. *Early Human Development, 19*, 9–19.

Van den Bergh, B. R. H., Mulder, E. J. H., Mennes, M., & Glover, V. (2005). Antenatal maternal anxiety and stress and the neurobehavioral development of the fetus and child: Links and possible mechanisms. A review. *Neuroscience & Biobehavioral Reviews, 29*, 237–258.

Van den Bergh, B. R. H., Van Calster, B., Smits, T., Van Huffel, S., & Lagae, L. (2008). Antenatal maternal anxiety is related to HPA-axis dysregulation and self-reported depressive symptoms in adolescence: A prospective study on the fetal origins of depressed mood. *Neuropsychopharmacology, 33*, 536–545.

Van Der Vaart, H. (1907). Children in the glass works of Illinois. In *National Child Labor Committee, Child labor and the republic*. American Academy of Political and Social Science. 78.

Viding, E., McCrory, E.J. (2018). Understanding the development of psychopathy: Progress and challenges. *Psychological Medicine, 48*, 566–577

Wallace, A. R. (1893a). Are individually acquired characters inherited? *Fortnigthly Review, 53*, 490–498; 655–668. https://people.wku.edu/charles.smith/wallace/S468.htm.

Wallace, A. R. (1893b). The non-inheritance of acquired characters. *Nature, 1893*, 267. https://people.wku.edu/charles.smith/wallace/S473.htm.

Wallace, A. R. (1893c). Prenatal influences on character. *Nature*, 389–390 https://people.wku.edu/charles.smith/wallace/S476.htm.

Waller, R., Hyde, L.W., Klump, K.L., & Burt, A., (2018). Parenting is an environmental predictor of callous-unemotional traits and aggression: A monozygotic twin differences study. *Journal of the American Academy of Child & Adolescent Psychiatry, 57*(12), 955-963. https://www.sciencedirect.com/science/article/abs/pii/S0890856718318677?via%3Dihub.

Wang, J.X., Kurth-Nelson, Z., Kumaran, D., Tirumala, D., Soyer, H., Leibo, J.Z., Hassabis, D., & Botvinick, M. (2018). Prefrontal cortex as a meta-reinforcement learning system. *Nature Neuroscience, 21*, 860-868.

Wang J.X., Kurth-Nelson, Z., Tirumala, D., Soyer, H., Leibo, J.Z., Munos, R., Blundell, C., Kumaran, D., Botvinick, M., (2016). *Learning to reinforcement learn.* Cornell University. https://arxiv.org/abs/1611.05763.

Warburton, R. (2019). *U.S. mass shootings: Just the facts.* ECORI. https://www.ecori.org/public-safety/2019/9/6/us-mass-shootings-just-the-facts

Watson, J. B., & Rayner, R. (1920). Conditioned emotional reactions. *Journal of Experimental Psychology, 3,*1–14.

Watson, E. J. (1910, January, 13-16). Enforcement of child labor laws. Lecture, annual meeting of the *National Child Labor Committee, Boston.*

Weaver, I. C. G., Cervoni, N., Champagne, F. A., D'Alessio, A. C., Sharma, S., Seckl, J. R., Meaney, M. J. (2004). Epigenetic programming by maternal behavior. *Nature Neuroscience, 7,* 847–854.

Weinstock, M. (2008). The long-term behavioural consequences of prenatal stress. *Neuroscience & Biobehavioral Reviews, 32,* 1073–1086.

Wheatley, M.J. (2006). *Leadership and the new science: Discovering order in a chaotic world.* Berrett-Koehler Publishers, Inc.

Williams, C. (1987). *The destruction of Black civilization.* Third World Press.

Wills, M. (2017). *When forced sterilization was legal in the U.S..* JS-TOR Daily. https://daily.jstor.org/when-forced-sterilization-was-legal-in-the-u-s/

Wisconsin Child Labor Committee, (1907). Report of the Wisconsin Child Labor Committee. In *National Child Labor Committee, Child labor and the republic.* (p. 157). American Academy of Political and Social Science.

Wood, M. E. (2011). *Emancipating the child laborer: children, freedom, and the moral boundaries of the market in the United States, 1853–1938* [Unpublished dissertation doctoral dissertation] University of Chicago.

Wood, S. B. (1968). *Constitutional politics in the Progressive Era: Child labor and the law.* University of Chicago Press.

Wooddy, C. H. (1935, May). Education and propaganda. *The Annals of the American Academy of Political and Social Science,* 179 Pressure Groups and Propaganda, 227-239. Sage Publications in association with the American Academy of Political and Social Science. https://www.jstor.org/stable/1020300?seq=1#page_scan_tab_contents

World Health Organization (2019). *Suicide.* https://www.who.int/news-room/fact-sheets/detail/suicide

Yehuda, R., Bierer, L. M., Schmeidler, J., Aferiat, D. H., Breslau, I., & Dolan, S. (2000). Low cortisol and risk for PTSD in adult offspring of holocaust survivors. *The American Journal of Psychiatry, 157,* 1252-1259.

Yehuda, R., Halligan, S. L., & Bierer, L. M. (2001). Relationship of parental trauma exposure and PTSD to PTSD, depressive and anxiety disorders in offspring. *Journal of Psychiatric Research, 35*, 261-270.

Yehuda, R., Blair, W., Labinsky, E., & Bierer, L. M. (2007). Effects of parental PTSD on the cortisol response to dexamethasone administration in their adult offspring. *The American Journal of Psychiatry, 164*, 163-166.

Zajenkowski, M. & Gignac, G.E. (2018). Corrigendum to "Why do angry people overestimate their intelligence? Neuroticism as a suppressor of the association between Trait-Anger and subjectively assessed intelligence Intelligence," *Intelligence, 70* (2018) 12–21. https://doi.org/10.1016/j.intell.2018.07.003.

Zamenhof, S., van Marthens, E., & Grauel, L. (1971). DNA (cell number) in neonatal brain: Second generation (F2) alteration by maternal (F0) dietary protein restriction. *Science, 172*, 850–851.

Zeanah, C.H., Egger, H.L., Smyke, A.T., Nelson, C.A., Fox, N.A., Marshall, P.J., & Guthrie, D. (2009). Institutional rearing and psychiatric disorders in Romanian preschool children. *The American Journal of Psychiatry, 166*(7), 777-785.

Zelizer, V. A. (1994). *Pricing the priceless child: the changing social value of children*. Princeton University Press.

Zerbi, V., Floriou-Servou, A., Markicevic, M., De Deyn, P.P., Wenderoth, N., Bohacek, J., von Ziegler, L., Ferrari, K.D., Weber, B., Vermeiren, Y., Sturman, O., & Privitera, M. (2019).

Rapid reconfiguration of the functional connectome after chemogenetic locus coeruleus activation. *Neuron, 103*(4), 702-718.